YANKEE D

YANKEE DROVER

Being the Unpretending Life of
ASA SHELDON,
Farmer, Trader, and Working Man
1788–1870

Foreword by
JOHN SEELYE

UNIVERSITY PRESS OF NEW ENGLAND
Hanover and London

UNIVERSITY PRESS OF NEW ENGLAND
Brandeis University
Brown University
Clark University
University of Connecticut
Dartmouth College
University of New Hampshire
University of Rhode Island
Tufts University
University of Vermont

Originally published as *Life of Asa G. Sheldon: Wilmington Farmer. In Two Arrangements*, by E. T. Moody, Woburn, Mass., 1862.
Copyright © 1988 by University Press of New England

Printed in the United States of America
∞

Library of Congress Cataloging-in-Publication Data

Sheldon, Asa, 1788–1870.
  Yankee drover.

  Rev. ed. of: Life of Asa G. Sheldon. 1862
  1. Sheldon, Asa, 1788–1870. 2. Massachusetts—
Biography. 3. Farmers—Massachusetts—Biography.
4. Labor and laboring classes—Massachusetts—History—
19th century. I. Sheldon, Asa, 1788–1870. Life of
Asa G. Sheldon. II. Title.
CT275.S462A3 1988   974.4'03'0924 [B]   88-229

ISBN 0–87451–439–8

5 4 3 2 1

CONTENTS

FOREWORD

I am a sojourner in old bookstores, where I find the materials of my trade. One Sunday, not long ago, in the company of a fellow member of the American Antiquarian Society, an institution whose purpose is the acquisition of old books, I traveled along Route 5 in the Upper Valley of Vermont, just across the river from New Hampshire, in search of dusty treasure. Jack was looking for rarities, chapbooks for children published in America before 1830, but I was more omnivorous. As a result, perhaps, I was the luckier one. Among the volumes we packed into his car, discovered in one of those emporia characteristic of New England enterprise, selling not only old books but new fishing gear and antique clothing, was what seemed at the time an interesting but not necessarily unique book, the *Life of Asa G. Sheldon: Wilmington Farmer*. Published in Woburn, Mass., in 1862, clearly at the expense of the author, it was an unprepossessing object: battered and shaken at the spine, the cloth cover torn at its hinges, but all the wear marks suggested use more than abuse, the edges of the pages having lost their corners through much turning. And the frontispiece, a portrait of the author taken from a photograph, put forth such a strong face that I was intrigued to see what lay within.

Now self-published autobiographies make up a small but determined genre in the United States, most of them religious in nature, often written by elderly ministers or their relicts in the hope of eking out a miniscule retirement stipend by advancing the cause of spiritual improvement. Some, a precious few, are the work of simpler folk, a prose equivalent to "primitive" paintings. Some years ago, Walter Teller, a tireless chronicler of Yankee characteristics, gathered a dozen of these "naive" autobiographies, at once establishing the genre and bottling the cream. Most of the narratives he assembled are of the "life and hard times" variety, like the tiny pamphlet written by Nancy Luce of Martha's Vineyard, with a photograph of the author and one of her favorite hens pasted onto the flyleaf. Miss Luce specialized in long poems about her chickens and composed prose anecdotes listing her physical ailments. Toward the end of her wretched life, she had become a landmark curiosity, the object of pilgrimage for summer visitors to the island, a phenomenon that only those who have spent an entire summer there can comprehend. She was a zany and skirted being hanged for a witch by a narrow two hundred years. But in the enlightened nineteenth century, zanies no longer had to entrust their lives to Cotton Mather: they had access to the press themselves, where they could air their persecutions, real or imagined, instead of being hauled into court and then yanked into heaven.

My first impression was that Asa G. Sheldon would be either one of the pious or the paranoid, but on looking further into the book, I began to find passages that suggested otherwise. I bought the book, therefore, and several evenings later spent the few hours it took to read Sheldon's story once through lightly. The more I read, the more convinced I became that he had written something superior to the usual thing. It was several rungs above the kind of home-built Jacob's ladder composed in the hope of rising above the mass of unwashed, unsung Miltons who lift their granite slabs skyward from hundreds of country graveyards in New England. Asa G. Sheldon was obviously *sui generis*, one of a kind, not so much perhaps in the details of his life — though there too he was remarkable — but in his ability to record those details in a clear, uncluttered, highly readable prose. He was therefore a capable spokesman for the legions of nineteenth-century New England farmers whose final testaments are often at best diaries recording weather and crops or, more likely, undecipherable ledger entries for miscellaneous financial transactions of a distinctly small order. Sheldon was both typical and singular. In the following pages, I hope to show why, although, as the rest of the book will demonstrate, he is quite capable of telling his own story.

At the moment of its founding, the United States was conceived by most of the men responsible for the act of independence as a nation of farmers. Chief among them was Thomas Jefferson, whose *Notes on the State of Virginia* is famous for championing the farming life as an ideal existence, as opposed to the oppressive conditions imposed on factory workers by the industrial revolution. Jefferson drew his ideology from the physiocrats of mid-eighteenth-century France, and he but gave the most famous expression to ideas held in common by many of his contemporaries. Even Alexander Hamilton, with whom we associate the promotion of industrial growth in the new republic, acknowledged the primacy of agriculture for the immediate future. One of the first books on the new United States published in Europe was Crèvecoeur's *Letters from an American Farmer* (1782), a physiocratic text entirely in harmony with Jefferson's philosophy. Based on the author's experience during a decade of residence in North America, the book traced the "New Man's" feelings of independence to his ownership of the land he tilled. In *The Virgin Land*, the foremost modern historian of our popular culture, Henry Nash Smith, has chronicled the overwhelming prevalence of the pastoral ideal in the United States. His student, Leo Marx, has demonstrated in *The Machine in the Garden* the extent to which that ideal pervades our literature.

But, as Smith observed, the farmer as an ideal figure in

the landscape did not provide much inspiration for *belles lettres*. Although the pastoral life has been praised by writers since the days of Virgil, as a mode of existence it seldom is characterized by the kinds of events that attract literary interest. Virgil himself created a highly idealized Roman shepherd in his Arcadian poems, so busy writing songs and courting shepherdesses as to find little time for sheep. Virgil's *Georgics* were written in praise of rural life, but they attract readers by rendering a detailed account of the rituals of farming as practiced in the time of Caesar Augustus, not by the "story" they tell, for there is none. And Crèvecoeur, having devoted an initial chapter to the joys of the farmer's life, thenceforth keeps the interest of his reader by conducting him on a tour of notable places in the colonies. He ends by letters by sending his ideal farmer into the wilderness terrain that would, according to Henry Nash Smith, prove to be the chief inspiration of most American writers of the nineteenth century, from Fenimore Cooper on. Jefferson, likewise, devotes much of the latter part of his *Notes* to a description of the western regions watered by the Mississippi and Missouri rivers, territory at the time still in the hands of Spain, but in which Jefferson read the future of the United States. Tending one's garden may be a rewarding activity, but writers from Milton to Voltaire have used it at the start or at the end of their stories, not as the main support of the action.

Leo Marx, in his study of the pastoral ideal in American literature, draws similar conclusions. Though a number of our nineteenth-century classics have rural settings, farmers have but minor and not always supporting roles to play. If, as Marx maintains, taking his map from Crèvecoeur, the ideal landscape in American literature is the "middle" zone, midway between the urban and wilderness regions, the emphasis of much American literature is on the outward passage into the wilderness, although the hero will ever and again return to the middle landscape. As

Mark Twain demonstrates in *The Adventures of Tom Sawyer*, St. Petersburg may connote a kind of heaven, but heaven can be a very dull place. Thus Twain's riverside village is generally portrayed as an oppressive, conformist zone from which his young heroes are forever escaping into exotic regions of pure adventure. Even Thoreau, celebrating the inspirational simplicity of the pastoral life in *Walden*, is careful to distinguish between the life he led beside his pond and that of the farmers who drew their subsistence, not essays, from the acres adjoining his plot. "John Farmer," as Thoreau called him, was a dull and unimaginative fellow, epitomized by the drover who got up before dawn to drive his oxen to market at Brighton Fair, so absorbed in his commercial errand as to be blind to the light that broke over the eastern hills toward which he and his equally dull beasts were plodding. Clearly a distinction was being made by these American writers between the ideal promise of rural life in America and the often grim reality.

Though the "voice" of the farmer was employed by physiocratic writers like Crèvecoeur or revolutionary propagandists like John Dickinson, in plain truth our literary annals contain very few actual farmer-authors whose main living came from tilling the land. An exception might be the popular nineteenth-century writer Donald G. Mitchell ("Ik Marvel"), best known for his sentimental sketches in *Dream Life* and *Reveries of a Bachelor*, who subsequently wrote a number of volumes about his experiences as a Connecticut farmer. Still, Mitchell was a sophisticated agricultural experimentalist, hardly a simple agrarian. How welcome it is therefore to come upon the autobiography of a very real farmer, whose life story brackets the first phase of the American republic.

Born in 1788 in Lynnfield, Massachusetts, near Salem, Asa Goodell Sheldon spent most of his life in the region of his birth, and identified himself in his biography as a resident of Wilmington, a small town less than fifty miles from the place of his birth. In this, as in many ways, Farmer Sheldon is a substantial shadow of Thoreau, who claimed to have traveled much in Concord, and by shadow I mean an image cast darkly upon the ground. As a Yankee farmer, Sheldon was just the kind of man Thoreau railed against, dedicated to getting ahead in the world, trudging behind his plow and team but never scratching deeper than was necessary to plant his next crop. But if the life of Asa Sheldon as recalled by himself confirms Thoreau's image of his neighbors, it also lends that shadow figure a glory undetected by the squatter on Emerson's land. In his own right, Farmer Sheldon puts forth an ideal, a substantial shape and counterpart to Thoreau's pastoral abstractions. His *Life*, published in the year of Thoreau's death, survives to haunt us all with its stone-simple and rock-hard memorial to the reality of a farmer's life during the first half of the nineteenth century.

First of all, as the preface and opening pages of his book suggest, Sheldon took as his model not Henry David Thoreau but that quintessential Yankee apostle of common sense, Benjamin Franklin, whose autobiography he occasionally quotes and whose spirit pervades his own life. For Sheldon was merely a Wilmington Farmer, no more than Ben was merely a Philadelphia Printer. At times a drover, a teamster, a sawmill operator, a stoneworker, railroad builder, earth mover, inventory, even for a time a state representative, Sheldon mirrors on his own level the ambidexterity of his great model. Just as the many-sided Franklin preferred the title of "Printer," that being a trade intimate with his self-image as a man of letters, so Asa Sheldon thought of himself as a Farmer, though much of his autobiography is devoted to matters other than the routines of the agricultural life. If, on the one hand, he thereby proves Henry Nash Smith's point about the unliterary qualities of farming, he also demonstrates an undeniable fact, namely that few farmers in the nineteenth century were able to make a living by raising crops and herds alone. There is still in my family a chest of cabinet-makers' tools owned by Morgan Seelye, a Connecticut contemporary of Sheldon, attesting to the way in which my own ancestor supplemented an income wrested from New England's obdurate soil.

Sheldon also proves that the life of a farmer need not be, contra Thoreau, a boring round of stultifying routines. His life story hardly challenges those highly colored autobiographies "written" by Daniel Boone and Davy Crockett, whose adventures helped make the frontier our ideal mythic zone. But he does show that one need not devote a career to destroying bears and Indians in order to have an interesting story to tell. At least three times Sheldon was nearly killed in accidents related to his various callings, one of which seems to have been an attempt on his life, and his several business trips to New York City and beyond were occasionally darkened by near scrapes with thugs. More important, by mastering that narrative technique Franklin praised in Bunyan and Defoe, mixing dialogue with discursive prose, Sheldon holds the reader's interest. Starting with a struggle of wills with the farmer to whom his father "sold" his services (suggesting that one did not have to be black in nineteenth-century America to know what bondage was), down to his fight with the Boston and Maine railroad over the wages due him, Sheldon shows us that the life of a farmer, boy and man, was hardly dull, nor, despite the ideal proposed by Jefferson and Crèvecoeur, was it one of unalloyed tranquility.

Most rewarding, however, to the modern reader are Sheldon's accounts of his business transactions, whether a simple trade of ox teams — equivalent to that classical image of the horse-swapping Yankee — or closing deals involving what were for the time large considerations of labor and cash. Much of the drama and humor in Franklin's autobiography comes from similar material — setting a

line of type after all is no more exciting than hoeing a row
of beans. Sheldon's negotiations were much more humble
— but no less fascinating. Seldom going "to law," sharing
his contemporaries' aversion for the needless expense and
time eaten up by lawyers, Sheldon was content with contracts made by the spoken word. His many anecdotes not
only give us a vivid picture of the commercial life of
nineteenth-century farmers and small entrepreneurs (for
such Sheldon increasingly became, contracting jobs and
hiring his own help), but they lend his narrative a high de-
gree of local color and humor. Although Yankee farmers
eked out their incomes with such transactions, the verbal
maneuvering involved was something to be savored.

Sheldon remains throughout his narrative very much a
man of small towns. Except for his few trips to New York
and other "southern" cities — occasioned by the sudden
wave of prosperity brought by the War of 1812 — and his
sojourn in Boston during one of his most ambitious projects
— the lowering of Pemberton Hill — Sheldon's activities
seldom took him to towns larger than Salem. For the most
part his business kept him moving along well-traveled but
hardly major thoroughfares, those roads crisscrossing the
regions north of Boston. The men with whom he mostly
dealt were likewise of modest station, with the exception of
the Baldwin family, that clan of early civil engineers. Even
today the Baldwins retain a certain fame, having built one
of the first canals in North America — the one that facili-
tated Thoreau's excursion on the Concord and Merrimack
rivers — and having laid down one of the region's (and the
nation's) first rail lines. Yet Farmer Sheldon was equally
impressed by the Baldwins' connection with one of New
England's best known apples, and, more to the literary
point, he tells a story about Loammi Baldwin and the sal-
vation of a towering, landmark pine tree that reveals the
connection found in so many writings by New Englanders
between considerations of beauty and utility. Characteristi-
cally, where Thoreau thought of the pine tree as a spiritual

symbol, Sheldon's sparing of the "King" tree was calculated to earn him a few more dollars.

Sheldon's accomplishments building railroads hardly challenge the Baldwins's fame, being matters of executing the designs of others, though he does seem to have devised better ways of laying down gravel beds, spacing ties, and building stone abutments. Nevertheless, Sheldon claims for himself a small but important place in the history of early American technology by his invention of wagon springs and an improved method of fastening wagon axles to their beds (devices incorporated in early automobiles also). His claim may be contested as yet another instance of contemporaneous invention, but Sheldon's sincerity cannot be doubted. Nor can his claim that his invention was spurred by painful necessity, in the case of the wagon spring (and similar springs supporting the wagon seat) impelled by what seems to have been an acute case of piles. Certainly the annals of utility can yield no more poignant example of inspiration.

Perhaps a modern reader may find this autobiography lacking in anecdotes of a personal kind, the flashes of intimacy that can illuminate psychological depths. Sheldon tells us that his father was a kindly, admirable man, but then alludes to his death merely in passing. He narrates one story about his aged mother and the apple trees she had him plant, but that is all, and having stated that his marriage was an important event, he never again mentions his wife or refers to whatever family life they had together. It is almost *all business*, yet again confirming Thoreau's negative image of the New England farmer. Still, Sheldon's model was Ben Franklin, who also tells us very little about his family life. And for all of Thoreau's expatiating on close personal relationships, in his writing we find very little that is intimate or revealing. Some of this we may attribute to reticence — a strong element in the Yankee character — but more important is the matter of intention.

Both Franklin and Thoreau were addressing themselves to their fellow Americans in the hope of bettering their lives, improving not family relationships but man's relations with the worlds of business and nature, respectively. As Sheldon's model was Franklin's book, his autobiography was written in that highly didactic tradition, summed up by the stated hope, in his Preface, that he would "add a mite of experimental knowledge to this age of improvement." He therefore related those aspects of his life that he felt would be of some practical use to his readers, whether those "boys" to whom he addresses asides during the account of his own youth or the "young men" to whom he speaks at later points in his narrative. Even if he had thought of telling more stories about his mother or the chief events of his married life, Sheldon's stated intention would have stopped him from going further.

We need to pause for a moment to consider Sheldon's phrase, "this age of improvement," because it is central to his book, providing both substance and motive. Writing with the intention of "improving" the next generation, Sheldon draws lessons from his own experiences promoting those "improvements" that characterize his day. The years during which Sheldon came to middle age — that is, the period that likewise saw the maturing of the Republic — witnessed what seemed at the time incredibly rapid advances in technology. The steamboat was perfected in 1807, and within ten years eastern waters were crowded with paddle-driven traffic; the completion of the Erie Canal in 1825 literally changed the shape of the American map; and the introduction of the steam locomotive in the 1830s not only challenged the steamboat's hegemony but in time put many canals out of business, including the one built by the Baldwins. When politicians like Daniel Webster spoke of "improvements," these were the things they meant, and they often coupled the word with another: "internal." Internal improvements included not only canals and rail lines but the removal of obstructions to navigation and the building of an extensive network of roads.

Webster and other Whig politicians usually linked internal improvements to the strengthening of the Union by lines of communication, but they also reckoned their importance by the growth of American industry and the increase in the rate of speed with which commerce — business — could be conducted. Clearly, Sheldon saw his own career as one closely related to the spread of those kinds of improvements. It is small wonder that he took pride in his modest contribution to a great epoch of progress. Thoreau, by contrast, makes ironic mention in *Walden* of the phrase "internal improvements," suggesting that Americans needed to make improvements of a much more profoundly "internal" kind — namely in matters of the spirit — before concerning themselves with railroads and the like. Asa Sheldon's notion of improvement never takes this transcendental track, but even Thoreau could thrill to the adventurous aspects of commerce, whether figured in the lives of boatmen on the Merrimack or as the destination of freight being carried close by his pond on the Fitchburg Railroad.

Sheldon seldom mentions what was being carried on those rails he laid from Boston to Lowell, yet between the 1820s and 1830s railroads switched from horse-drawn cars to steam power, a revolutionary change. Like Thoreau's ox drover, Sheldon seems indeed to have kept his eyes on the ground, but that, once again, is his chief value to us. We have many contemporary accounts of the excitement people felt when beholding a steam train, but only Sheldon tells us how the stones were laid in the abutments that made train travel possible. Thoreau was grimly ironical about the "sleepers" that lay under the iron rails, but for Sheldon they were simply "ties," and he regarded cedar as the best wood for such a purpose. Thoreau relished in sarcastic detail the expenses entailed in building his hut and farming his lot. For Sheldon these were serious matters, and his delight comes from relating how he learned that stones for building could be more easily dragged over the ground if slid upon straw or how he bested a city slicker who thought to "shave a Yankee."

In the end, however, there is a concurrence between *Walden* and Sheldon's life story. Thoreau's book ends with his famous description of the melting mud on a railroad embankment in springtime, evincing the triumph of life over death and nature over man's technology. Sheldon ends with the story of his disastrous dealings with the Boston and Maine, a struggle that resulted in the loss of all his money and property. Despite the corporation's maneuverings, Sheldon stuck to his sense of justice and won. The money was eaten up by his creditors, who descended on him when word got out that the railroad had refused Sheldon what was owed, an episode common in the days of nineteenth-century commerce, where so much business dealing depended on personal credit, which often far exceeded real collateral. But Sheldon had made his point and had also exercised his American right to protest in print his treatment by the railroad corporation: his only other published work is a pamphlet directed to the directors of the Boston and Maine corporation. Sheldon may have been Thoreau's antithesis, but he was hardly one of the "sleepers" who allowed themselves to be run over in silence by the railroad. To quite different ends, then, both books conclude with the same subject, the railroad, the presence and impact of which changed the destiny of the United States forever. It is a moot point as to the prescience of the two endings, Thoreau's poetic evocation of the victory of nature over man's creation or Sheldon's angry denunciation of the railroad's callous treatment of the men who created it.

While acknowledging that the Boston and Maine was ruinously unfair to Sheldon, we may still be grateful to that primitive corporation, for had it not attempted to cheat him out of his due, we may doubt that he ever would have written his autobiography. Despite Sheldon's reference to his intended audience at the start of his book, his declared hope of educating a younger generation, it seems clear that his autobiography was framed by a desire to square his account with the Boston and Maine by a work that would outlast his earlier pamphlet. His story falls into two parts or "arrangements." The first consists of the "links" that made up the chief events of his life. The second commences with a section called "Stone Work" and deals with his accomplishments laying stone, starting with an incident involving a single rock in 1809 and ending with the work he did for the Boston and Maine and his reward therefrom. Thus the first "arrangement" is the foundation for what follows, the carefully laid courses that establish his integrity and enterprise, bearing witness to the character of the man who labored so hard "for the corporation whose agent afterwards ruined me." We're not told Sheldon's political allegiance, but in his fight with the railroad as with his legislative quarrel with bankers who wished to raise the "usury" level past six percent, he reveals himself to be something of an early populist, pitting himself as a simple, hardworking, honest farmer against the power of corporations and banks.

If Thoreau can be seen as setting the radical style in the United States, opposing the authority of government by civil disobedience, then Sheldon should have a place also in our radical pantheon, aiming his anger not at the structure of government but at those capitalistic instruments to which the Constitution gave warrant. Thoreau finally found in Captain John Brown a "farmer" he could believe in. But Brown was inspired to move against slavery after a series of financial reverses like those Sheldon experienced: disappointments in real estate and commodity speculation connected with the monopolistic maneuvers of large corporations. Brown was able to associate his own misfortunes with the fate of black people, themselves victims of capi-

talism in its agrarian manifestation, the dark side of Jefferson's pastoral dream. Sheldon stopped far short of that
transfer, but in terms of American literature, his picture of
the simple farmer exploited by the railway looks forward to
the short stories of Hamlin Garland and Frank Norris's
The Octopus.

John Brown expressed his discontent in such dramatic
ways that Thoreau could see him as an American Cromwell
and a revolutionary, nor was Thoreau as he hoed his beans
at Walden unaware of those Concord ghosts who had far-
med the land before him. Despite his disclaimer, it was no
mere coincidence that Thoreau set up shop at Walden Pond
on the Fourth of July, for like those others he too was an
embattled farmer, waging war on the American materialis-
tic spirit. And Asa Sheldon, commencing his autobiography
by claiming descent from Israel Putnam on his mother's
side, ends by imitating that Yankee Cincinnatus, ratifying
the spirit of 1776 by taking on a corporation, the modern
equivalent to the British crown. If Sheldon's autobiography
of a "Yankee drover" is the antithesis to Thoreau's *Walden*,
then in the dialectic of American radicalism they merge in
a final synthesis, sharing in the glory of a New England
dawn.

The editor wishes to thank Mr. Richard Fyffe of the Essex
Institute for providing information used in this foreword.

Hanover, New Hampshire   J.S.
November 1987

PREFACE

To gratify the wishes of numerous friends, to indulge in living the past over again, to give what I may of encouragement to the temperate and diligent, to cheer the disheartened, amid the common trials of life, to give my voice of warning to the selfish and vicious, and to add a mite of experimental knowledge to this age of improvement, this unpretending autobiography is sent forth, hoping it may meet with the same kindly reception from friends and the community at large, as, for so many years, has its

AUTHOR.

❖ FIRST ARRANGEMENT ❖

FIRST LINK IN THE CHAIN OF LIFE

❖❖❖

I was born in Lynnfield, Mass., October 24th, 1788. My first recollections are of the domestic circle, in connection with parents, brothers and sisters.

My father, Jeremiah Sheldon, was son of Skelton Sheldon, and he a son of Godfrey Sheldon, the first on record in this country. He was a man of uniform cheerfulness, and sweet, even temper. I do not remember his ever speaking a cross word to me. In writing, he possessed an uncommon tact, and in the capacity of clerk attended Judge Houghton several years in Congress, then sitting in Philadelphia.

My mother's name was Elizabeth Goodell, of English extract on the maternal side, whose parents emigrated from the Isle of Barbadoes with seventeen slaves. On her father's side she was direct descendant from General Putnam, who commanded in the memorable battle of Bunker Hill, on June 17, 1775, where brave Warren fell. Like her world-renowned ancestor, she possessed indomitable energy and perseverance. The plan once formed, like Putnam when he shot the "Wolf in his den," was carried out with a determination of purpose that brings an unfailing reward. Their children were —

> ELBRIDGE, born Nov. 18th, 1781, married Eleanor Harding.
>
> LUCINDA, born Aug. 7, 1783, married John Howard.
>
> SAMUEL HOUGHTON, born Dec. 26, 1786, married Sally French.

ASA GOODELL, born Oct. 1788, married Clarissa
    Eames.
HARRIET, born Aug. 5, 1791.
BETSEY, born Dec. 16, 1795.
JEREMIAH, born Jan 26, 1798, married an
    English lady in South America.
SOPHIA, born Aug. 24, 1801, married Joseph R.
    Hathaway.

In my mother was strikingly exemplified King Solomon's
wise woman, who "seeketh wool and flax, and worketh willingly with her hands."

For many years she entered largely into the domestic
manufacture of blue and white striped woollen Frocking,
then generally used by farmers, teamsters and butchers;
and so slow were the inroads made by time on her vigorous
constitution, that she was able to follow that business until
within four years of her death, which occurred at the advanced age of 94 years and 41 days. When in her 90th year
she prepared a web with her own hands, for which she
realized a premium from the Agricultural Society, at the
Cattle Show at Concord, Mass. When 88 years of age, she
expressed a desire to have four apple trees set for her. To
comply with her request, I selected those that promised to
bear young, and sent a man to set them. Previous to his
coming she had driven four stakes in the four corners of her
garden and marked the circumference of the holes she
wished made. This made ready, she held the tree and gave
directions for placing the roots and had all done to her ap-
proval. She lived to eat fruit from two of them. Let no aged
person be discouraged about setting fruit trees. Set the tree
if you have opportunity, and if you never eat its fruit, let the
deed be ascribed to *disinterested benevolence.*

> As wave chases wave o'er the ocean's dark breast,
> So the races of men pass on to their rest;
> Be this our endeavor, with purpose sublime,
> Some footprints to leave on the quicksands of time.

Well do I remember, in the days of my childhood, the first copper ever earned with my own hands. It was by opening a gate for Mrs. Sherman, a lady on horseback, — a very common mode of riding in those days. She told me to keep it, and she would give me a box to keep it in. The next day I received a tin box with the promise of a copper every time I would open the gate for her or her husband, when they were on horseback; which promise was faithfully kept, and oftentimes to my great joy two coppers jingled into the box instead of one. At that time coppers were the only copper currency extant, — 108 of them making $1, — and our cents took their place. The possession of the tin box created a strong desire to have it filled. Some, on seeing the box and contents, would drop in one or two coppers, while others needed urging to do so; and with pleasure I saw it filling up more rapidly than I had anticipated. It was soon found to contain money enough to buy me a pewter porringer out of which to eat bread and milk in the summer, and broth and bean porridge in the winter season; and a primer to study the Assembly's Catechism in.

The arrangement being made by my mother, I went to pedlar John Parker's, about a half mile distant, to make the purchase, my sister Lucinda accompanying me. This was the first time I had ever made so large a purchase, and the honest pedlar, seeing he had taken my last copper, gave me a tin whistle. Like Dr. Franklin, when a child, "I went home whistling." I would here say to boys, be careful of noisy amusements within doors; you little know how much it annoys parents and seniors, whose heads are filled to overflowing with the cares and perplexities of life. Well do I remember how much my mother was tried with my whistle. I was proud enough of my shining porringer, and the possession of such a treasure gave more satisfaction than many dollars in after life.

When between three and four years of age Miss Sherman came into our house and said to mother, "Why they *do say* Daniel Hart is courting Polly Tapley." I was very anxious for her departure, wishing to know what Daniel Hart was doing to Polly Tapley.

"Mother," said I, as soon as Miss Sherman was gone, "what is Daniel Hart doing to Polly Tapley."

"What do you mean," said mother.

"Why, Miss Sherman said he was courting her."

"Oh, he is coaxing her to be his wife," said mother.

Anon this couple were married, she still living at her father's, and in April, 1793, Mr. Hart was presented with a son.

I was much at home at neighbor Tapley's, and was soon asked to see the baby.

"Where did you get that baby," said I.

"The Doctor brought it," said she.

"What did you give for it?" was the next question.

"If I like it well enough to keep it I shall give $5," was the answer.

"Why do you lie there in bed?"

"To keep it warm," said she.

Daniel Hart and Polly Tapley raised up six sons, — David, Daniel, Aaron, Elijah, William and Tapley.

These six sons have all been in my employ, — five of them at one time, when the Boston and Lowell Railroad was in process of construction. It has become a proverb, that "all Hart's boys were born with a whip in their hand." Certainly I should not know where to find six men, possessed of so good faculties to manage oxen and horses, as those six brothers. And it appears this faculty has not passed away yet, for the last time I was going to Boston, I met four beautiful horses with a large load of manure, driven by Charles C. Hart, son of D. D. Hart, and great grandson to Daniel Hart and Patty Tapley. It seemed to be moving along with as much ease and comfort as a lady at work sitting in her parlor rocking-chair.

This brings to mind six generations of that race of people,

since I came upon the stage of action, Gilbert Tapley of Danvers; Joseph Tapley of Lynnfield; Polly Tapley, daughter of Joseph Tapley; David Hart, son of Daniel Hart and Polly Tapley; David Dexter Hart, of Woburn, and Charles Choate Hart, his son. I would say to the sixth generation, that it is my hope to live to see the seventh.

Being now in my fifth year, and having often heard rivers spoken of, my young heart was filled with curiosity to see such a flow of water. So one day, having obtained leave of mother, brother Samuel — who was two or three years older than myself — and I started for Ipswich River, about a mile and a half distant. On the way we stopped at a house, where we were joined by three other boys, strangers to me. The two eldest were Samuel and Osgood Flint, the youngest was Samuel Gilford, who was about my own age. We arrived at the River at the spot were it divides Lynnfield from North Reading and were a bridge has since been built, about fifty rods from the East Schoolhouse. The oldest boys then went in swimming, while Gilford and myself amused ourselves by muddying our feet and legs and then sitting on a shelving place on the bank and washing them. This was done several times, but now the sport assumed a more serious character, for as I was sitting unconscious of danger, Gilford run up behind and pushed me into the River, where the water was over my head. Just at this critical moment the other boys looking round, saw Gilford running toward home, and the Flints, knowing him to be a bad boy, cried out, "Asa is in the River," and came with all possible haste to my rescue, and with great exertion soon laid me on dry land, safe and sound. All the boys in the neighborhood despised Sam Gilford for that trick until the family moved away, and a good riddance it was. What became of him, I know not. I wish my young readers, both male and female, to take warning by this vicious boy, who was hated by all who knew him, and not indulge in any sport that may lead to the disadvantage or unhappiness of others. No doubt, in this case, the evil may be traced back to parents and grandparents, whose vicious indulgence served to encourage rather than to amend wrong propensities.

My first contract made for a day's work, was with Mr. William Flint of North Reading, for the sum of 6¼ cts., and I received the cash at night, returning home highly pleased with so much money; besides much praise was given me by Mr. Flint, who said I had thrown half as many stones into the cart as he had, the stones being small. In justice to Mr. Joseph Tapley, I must say, my first instructions in farming and teaming came through his discipline. Sometimes he would give me a copper for cleaning out his cattle, and sometimes two for helping fill a load of manure, or riding horse to plow, or driving oxen, which suited me best of all work.

He employed me in spreading, turning and raking hay, hoeing corn and potatoes, &c.; in short he was always ready to let jobs at from one copper to 6¼ cts., and we always agreed upon the price before commencing the job, — a rule that should always be practiced whether dealing with men or boys.

My mother was always satisfied with the price paid. All the neighboring boys liked to work for him. He was a jovial man, and now, in after life, I look back on him as a great benefit to boys in that vicinity. One morning he said, "go and ask your mother if you may go to Lynn with me; tell her Jesse is going." Mother gave her consent, and we started with a yoke of oxen and span of horses. We went two miles, where we loaded the wood, we boys handing it up to him.

As we passed through Lynn woods we saw three persons cross the road ahead completely dressed in white. We boys were somewhat alarmed, and inquiringly asked who they were? Mr. T. saw our surprise, and answered that they might be white Indians, but if we would be good boys they would not hurt us. I am sorry I cannot inform my readers

who they were, but I never saw their like before or since. As
Mr. Tapley turned round, after delivering the wood, the
forward wheels dropped into the gutter breaking the bolt.
"Now boys," said Mr. Tapley, with affected surprise, "how
can you ride home?"

This was a sad question to us boys, and we began to cry,
for we were tired and had never been half as far from home
before.

"Now boys," said he, "stop crying and behave like men,
and take hold and help, and I will see if I can fix things so
as you may ride." We were soon on the way home, and called at a tavern about half a mile below where Lynnfield
Hotel now stands, and he bought four coppers worth of gingerbread, which was the first food I had ever eaten in a
tavern. This occurred between the ages of 6 and 7. Mr.
Tapley, as will be inferred, was a man full of jokes and fun,
yet a man of active mind and a benefactor of his race. It
was his delight to set boys to work and teach them how to
do it. He was great grandfather to David D. Hart, of
Woburn.

When 7 years of age, I made a contract with Clark &
Epps, of Lyndboro', N. H., and Col. Flint, of North Reading,
drovers, to drive their cattle and sheep from our house to
Jerre Upton's tavern, two miles distant, that they might
ride ahead and take breakfast while the drove came on, for
four coppers each trip, which occurred weekly. Boys, the
price may appear small, but in those days it was a good income. This was continued for two successive summers, the
last of which I commenced going to school.

Miss Hannah Sherman, relative of the lady who gave me
the tin box, was teacher. She had her scholars seated on
three wooden benches, so arranged that she could reach
each one with her long willow stick without rising from her
chair. Jesse Tapley was the best scholar in school. I had
commenced reading in the New Testament, and the old
lady was very urgent that I should read with him. This

suited me well, and the teacher, to bring it about, agreed that Jesse and I should occupy the same seat in one corner of the room, and to me was granted the privilege of whispering to Jesse to inquire out the hard words. We both studied hard, each trying to excel the other. Sometimes we would commit our whole lesson to memory. When mother would question me at home, I could sometimes relate all I had read during the day, and would ask her, "has God all power in heaven and earth and hell?" She answered, "He has." Said I, "did he always possess it?" She said, "he did." That night I slept but little, and the morning found my pillow wet with tears. Distress of mind followed me, and the talk soon became current that I was growing poor and should be kept from school. The lady who gave me the tin box came to our house and advised to that course, saying, "he is killing himself with study," she being highly interested in my case. I told them it would do no good to stay from school, but wished I could go to meeting, which was soon granted, and terrible appeared the sermon when the preacher gave it as his opinion that only one in ten were saved. I now felt worse than before, and thought it would have been better had I been born a calf, or lamb, or almost any other kind of beast, rather than a human being. My suffering was great, — an awful week to me. Every one appeared to think that I was about to die, but they knew not the cause of my trouble. It originated in reading the life and death of Jesus Christ, for I could not see the reason why God gave his Son to suffer and die for man, when he had all power in heaven and earth, and always had possessed that power.

The next Sabbath another minister preached, who quoted the opinion of an eminent divine, "that not more than one in a hundred would be saved." The fact which was here made apparent, that ministers disagreed upon the all-important subject, lightened my burden and made me feel more at ease. In conclusion, I would add, that it is my firm belief that God is holy, just and wise; that he possesses all power in heaven, earth and hell; that no one ever interrupted his plans, or ever can.

In the Spring of 1796, I was employed by the farmers to drive oxen to plough, — a work that always pleased me, — at a shilling per day, which supplied me with books and some clothing with which to attend school in summer and winter.

The winter previous I boarded with grandmother Sheldon, in Danvers, and attended a school kept by a Mr. Felton in a private house near Rope's Mill, now known as Phelp's Mill. I here formed an acquaintance with three noble brothers, — Ralph, Samuel and Lemuel Crane, the last named was near my age, and many a good piece of pie I received on his account.

Ralph died on the 15th of November, 1808, of nervous fever. Lemuel turned his attention to the sea, and on the 16th of February, 1808, he fell from the masthead of the ship Belisarius, of Salem, commanded by Capt. Benjamin Lovett, and was killed. Samuel became a highly respectable man, and now resides in South Danvers.

My father, owning but few acres of land, worked much of the time stoning wells and cellars, and consequently was with his family but little. Generally working in Salem, we saw but little of him, except on the Sabbath, yet I can distinctly remember his good-natured manners. I never knew him to speak unkindly to me, and very seldom to any one.

In December, 1796, my father purchased a lot of standing wood in North Reading, and being then in my ninth year, I was employed, in connection with a man, to drive a team with a very large yoke of cattle in dragging off the wood, the man driving another team.

Being very small for my age, it attracted some attention to see so small a boy beside a loaded team. It was the heighth of my ambition to become a teamster. Sometimes we turned our teams across the side of Putnam's Millpond, for the pleasure of driving on the glare ice. This made fun for the school children, who could then get a ride without paying fare. The method was for one or two boys to take hold of the hind end of the load, then a girl took hold of his clothes, and other hold of hers, and so on, till a long string was made out, oftentimes two strings, as the case might be. At one time, my companion laughingly said to me, "You load the oxen too heavy;" seeing a beautiful little girl behind, I said, "No, no, I will not leave the hind end."

SECOND LINK

We now come to an important period in the history of a youth,
— I refer to leaving home. What a privilege to parents it is,
to be able to employ their children at home, and thus keep
them around them under their careful scrutiny, and what a
blessed privilege to children to live under the care and
guidance of discreet parents.

On April 14th, 1797, being still in my ninth year, Mr.
David Parker came to my father's house to get a boy to live
with him. Mother said he might take his choice, Samuel or
Asa. "I will take Asa," he said, "because he is the youngest."

Accordingly, my father went over with me. It was a fine,
sunny day, but there was snow enough on the ground to
make good sleighing. We stopped on our way at Putnam's
saw mill, where, although so late in the Spring, I saw more
oxen and men engaged in drawing lumber than I ever saw
there before or since, at one time.

I commenced my servitude here without time or
remuneration being stated, which, as I before said, is a circumstance liable to produce difficulty.

I found the family to consist of Mr. Parker, who was
about 40 years of age, and wife, of nearly the same age;
David, about 18, and two daughters, Polly and Sally, who
were a few years younger. Mrs. Parker told me to call her
"mother," and certainly she acted the part of a mother to
me. She fed me when hungry; dried my clothes when wet;
cared for my every want; and when troubles assailed, that
she could not alleviate, pitied and sympathised with me. In
short, she was as kind as my own mother.

On first entering the house, I found no one at home but Mrs. Parker and her two daughters, David being absent at school. After sitting a few minutes, she said, "You may go to the barn and see the calves." There were six of them, and I employed the forenoon in cleaning the stalls and clearing up. After dinner I went with Mr. Parker to split oak butts into wheel spokes. Thus ended my first day's servitude.

Mr. Parker's parents were then living. His mother, by age or infirmity, had lost her reason, or, as it is commonly expressed, was crazy. They told me that she would not harm me, so I need not be afraid of her. I well remember her saying one day, "Asa, the Devil is in me." "Well," said I, "if he is, route him out," at the same time seizing the fire shovel. She blowed and coughed till tired, and seeing me not frightened, stopped, saying, "I can't blow him out." She reported, that she never saw a boy of such determined courage; "he was not afraid of the Devil himself, but stood ready to beat his brains out with the fire-shovel."

Our Spring ploughing that year was done by four oxen and a horse, and it was my constant business to drive them. In hoeing, the plan was for me to take every alternate hill and follow back on the same row, thus keeping alongside the men. The Summer passed pleasantly away, — my young head filled with a lively interest in everything that transpired on the farm. I had become quite attached to my new mother and Mr. Parker seemed quite a middling man to get along with.

I had the privilege of attending winter school, and as is common for youth, formed a lasting attachment to a schoolmate, — Daniel Putnam, a boy nearly my size and age, but of whom it might be said, as of Nathaniel of old, "an Israelite indeed, in whom is no guile." We occupied the same seat, and one day the teacher detected Daniel whispering to me, contrary to known laws. Of course, Dan was called to the floor, and seeing the teacher about to ferule him, I sprang from my seat, hastened forward, and holding out my hand, cried out, "punish me, I am more to blame than he; I whispered first."

"Was you ever punished at school?" said the teacher.

"No, sir," I answered.

"Was you ever, Daniel?"

"No, sir."

"Then," said he, in a authoritative tone, "go to your seats."

— The second year, in hoeing time, I was able to keep up with the hands, unless the ground was very tough. This pleased Mr. Parker as there was much hoeing to be done, and the crops were extensive.

My father needing a cow, he agreed with Mr. P. to take one for $22, and I was to work for him another year, or till the next May, to pay for her, and I was to have winter schooling.

Mr. P. appears to have been exceedingly miserly, and was unwilling to let me slide on the ice, because it wore my shoes out; but thanks to mother Parker's adroit management, I found frequent opportunities to enjoy an hour of glee on the ponds. For that and many other secret favors, I have reason to respect her memory.

— At the commencement of my third year, Mr. P. frequently urged that I should be bound to him, telling my father that he would give him $20 in cash, and me $100 on becoming twenty-one. To this my father agreed, and the necessary documents were signed without mother's knowledge. Great was her anguish on learning that her son was a "bond slave," as she was pleased to call it.

O fathers, never be guilty of such a rash act. Never bind your children to service of any kind, and above all without the consent of her who would willingly labor day and night; yea, and suffer many privations to benefit her offspring.

I am glad that this inhuman practice has passed away. Depend upon it, this generation is not *good* enough to deal in such a relic of barbarism.

— I now come to speak of my fourth year of service. There was no snow for sledding till February or March, when a nice fall of snow coming, created an ambition in me to drive a load of wood to Salem town and sell it. I had frequently driven wood to market in company with Mr. Parker, each of us driving a load. Mr. P., Dave and myself, were engaged at Putnam's Mill all day. It was late at night when they retired.

In my thirteenth year, full of ambition, I unloaded a sledload of boards, — they were heavy, hard pine boards, 22 feet in length, — and reloaded it with pine wood. It was now midnight, and I sought my accustomed couch, but tied my shoes so tight as to prevent quiet rest, and after an hour and a half's repose I rose and fed the team. Then going to Mr. P. the following dialogue took place:

"Can I take a load of wood to Salem today?"

"Asa, it seems as if you tease the life out of me; did I not tell you there was none loaded."

"But there is a load loaded."

"Who loaded it?"

"I loaded it," said I.

"Yes, you may go if you have got the wood loaded. You may unload it at Johnson's, where we get store goods, I have promised it to him."

A dash of disappointment flashed over me, for I longed to dispose of the wood myself. A pleasant trip brought me into Salem at 8 o'clock. I found Mr. Johnson absent, and his clerk would do nothing about it. Much pleased was I at this overture, which gave me an opportunity to try my luck at marketing. I was to get from Johnson $4 for the load, but had the good luck to sell it to a man for $4 and one shilling. On reaching home, Mr. Parker gave me the shilling, the greatest present he had ever made me. My spending money had before been confined to 6¼ cents per year. That was awarded to me at our State Election. The last year of my living with him he gave me 12½ cents. The man who bought the wood was a baker by trade, and proved a good customer for years afterwards when marketing wood for myself. The very boards which I that night unloaded solely myself, may now be found on the roof of Thomas Raynor's house, in North Reading.

When at Salem a baker agreed with me for a load of fagots, or twigs bound in bundles, for heating ovens. With the hope that Mr. Parker would give me all the money if I could contrive to make them without taking his time, I kept my hatchet in the cow pasture, and when I found the cows handily I could make eight or ten bundles and then run and catch up with them. If I did not find them readily, I made less, and so on. When the load was nearly complete, Mr. Parker discovered them, and asked, "Who made those fagots?"

"I made them," said I.

"When did you make them," said he, "and what are you going to do with them."

"Sell them," said I, "they will bring as much as a load of wood."

"You can't sell them for anything."

"Yes, I can, they are promised now."

"Well," said he, "finish out the load, now you have begun."

The day we finished haying, Mr. Parker said, "if you are going down with that load of fagots, you had better do it before we take the hay rigging off."

Mother P. had told me, that whenever I sold them, if he offered me less than a dollar, not to take it. I drove the load to Salem, and brought home $5.80, and gave it to Mr. Parker, and he was niggardly enough to offer me 12½ cents for all my labor, hurry and toil. Mother P., seeing me about to take it, gave a stamp with her foot, when the ninepence dropped on the floor, and I hastened out of the house. Soon after, Mother P. went to Salem herself and brought home a nice hat for me, that cost $3. There was but one other hat worn in town that was so nice, and that was owned by George, now Esquire, Flint, of North Reading. On presenting it she said, "There, Asa, that will do you more good than ninepence."

Polly Parker had been married to Thomas Raynor, and resided one year at South Reading. They then removed to our house to share in the profits of the farm, — Mr. Parker cultivating both his own and his father's farm. It appears from circumstances that Mr. Parker, at the time of his marriage, thought Tom Raynor was heir to an estate; but such not being the case, he seemed to look indignantly upon his son-in-law, and nothing suited that he laid his hands upon.

We all lived in one family, the men jointly sharing the profits of the farms. Mr. Parker had one half, Dave and Tom each one fourth. I have known them to divide $1200 at the end of the year.

The first time I ever came to Wilmington, was with a team loaded with hops, which I sold to Colonel William Blanchard for 42 cents per lb., amounting to $800.

— Now commenced my fifth year. In passing down one side the hay-field, one day, where Parker and Raynor were turning hay, I heard Parker shout to Raynor, "Why don't you turn that hay with the head of your rake?" Parker, receiving no answer or not being heard, shouted again in an angry tone, "if you can't turn the hay as I want you to, go home to dinner, and I will turn it." Raynor still not appearing to hear, and continuing to ply the stale of his rake, the old fellow ran upon him with his rake, and levelling a blow on his temple brought him to the ground. He fell as quick as ever an ox fell in a slaughter house.

I was frightened almost out of my senses, and ran toward them as fast as my legs would carry me. However, Raynor sprang up, and with rake in hand, exclaimed, "Stand off; I was never made to fear a fall of clay." They both appeared at the dinner table that day and ate without exchanging a word. From that time till the close of the year, they never spoke a word to each other, except when so filled with anger that they could not help spitting it out, yet they constantly ate and worked together. Parker always called Raynor a bad tempered man; but I knew them both well, and Raynor had not half so bad a temper as Parker himself.

Strange as it may seem, I was daily called to act as interpreter between them. Oftentimes when sitting by the fire, Parker would tell me what to say to Raynor, and he in return would tell me what to answer back. Sometimes the case would require quite a number of messages, and all this while they were sitting nearer to each other than I was to either of them. This curious telegraphing was sometimes carried on at table, especially when farm operations required each to know the other's mind. At such times one would not notice what the other said until I repeated it.

To my readers this may appear very strange and almost beyond credence, but it is a simple fact; and certain am I, that if I had not personally known the man, I could never have believed the one half I now know to be true. He was a man whose iron will completely blockaded every port of his enjoyment.

In the Spring of the year, it was Mr. Parker's practice to give me a stint stripping hop poles. Hop raisers, and perhaps others, will understand that process. This, he said, was to give me a chance to supply myself with spending money. I was grateful for the benefit, and am bound to say in his praise that he never gave a hard stint. At evening I was sometimes aided by neighboring boys, when a bonfire of the dried vines would increase the hilarity.

Once upon a time in April, the snow falling fast, Mr. Parker came to me and said, "if you will leave vine stripping and go and get the sheep up, I will pay you for it." I did, and found a wee little lamb dropped in the snow. Taking off my frock I wrapped it up and conveyed it home. "Now Asa," said Mr. Parker, "if you will make that lamb live, you may have it to pay for going after the sheep, and all the ewe lambs she has I will keep for you for their wool, and the male lambs you may sell to the butchers." All night I watched the wee bit and in the morning it was able to draw its own "rations" from its dam.

The coming season I exchanged my lamb for an older sheep, which brought me the next spring two fine ram lambs that were destined to the slaughter. However, my stock of sheep increased to five before I left the place, which I sold, receiving $10 for them.

It is but just to say in this place, that I made Mr. Parker my Savings Bank, putting all my little overplus in his keeping, and he giving me a new note every year, carefully reckoning compound interest. When I left he was owing me $30 saved in this manner. It was not till years afterwards that I demanded and received it.

Boys, here is an incentive to lay by your little savings. They will amount to something at a time when you need them.

THIRD LINK

Early in the autumn, the Frigate Essex was to be launched. All the boys in the neighborhood were going. I wanted to go, but Mr. Parker said no. And it was not till several boys had interceded with him that he gave his consent. "Well," said he, "if you do go, I will not give you one cent of money to spend, for there is no need of going." The boys said I should fare as well as they did.

We started at midnight, eighteen in all, and walked to Salem, saw the Essex leave "the home of her birth," and slide gently down the greased ways, with her precious cargo of curious mortals, anxious to catch the first ride in her as she bathed herself for the first time in the briny deep.

Afterwards we walked about town to see the "elephant," ate gingerbread and pies, and toward night set our faces toward home. It was a most formidable journey for boys of our age, and before we reached home our fatigue was such that we lay down on the ground to rest every half mile.

Boys, when distant from home, be cautious not to take too much labor upon yourselves. Remember you have got to travel home into the bargain. Such almost killing fatigue mars the pleasure of the otherwise satisfactory excursion.

In the following story, I have to acknowledge the first and only time I ever tried to plague Mr. Parker, and then I tried with a right-good will, for I was mad as a honey bee. He had fallen in the barn and hurt himself considerably, and had kept in the house for four days.

I was going to Salem with a load of wood, and had my team all hitched and ready, when he called to me to get Raynor up for the purpose of going a piece with me, as the snow was deep and drifted.

"I do not want him," said I.

"Go along and call him quick." The mandate was obeyed.

"Do *you* want me," said Raynor.

"No," said I.

"Then I shall not get up."

"Is he going to get up," said Parker.

"He said not."

"Then go and tell him I say he *shall* get up and go with you."

Again I ran and told him what Parker said. He asked me, "Do *you* want me to go? if you do, I will, but if you do not, I shall not get up."

This message was delivered *verbatim* to Parker, when he answered, "Did you tell him that *you* wanted he should go?"

"No, sir."

"Why didn't you?"

"Because if I did it would be a lie; and you always told me if I told a lie you would whip me, and I do not want him or any body else to go."

"Then," shouted he, "run quick to the other barn and get the white horse and I will go myself." And he did go.

Although he had required waiting upon for four days, he was up and dressed and mounted upon Old White, that cold night, for no other purpose than to carry out his iron will, formed to discomfort Raynor and get him out of bed that bitter night, — he so hated him, and in effect he imitated the vexed rattlesnake, who

> Missing his foe, with fiendish spite,
> Coils up his folds, and his own self will bite.

To be sure I was any thing but good natured, scampering away to the other barn for Old White, whose contrary habits were well known, sincerely hoping she would manifest something of the kind that night and plunge her rider in the snow. But I was not to be gratified in that respect. Old White was saddled, taken home, and a chair brought out for him to mount with, so lame was he from his hurt. He tried to ride ahead, but could not get on fast enough, for when he told me to drive slower in the drifts, I would use the brad unsparingly, making the team, which was a good one, rave and spring, but could not get him unhorsed with all the trick and tact I was master of. "You act so much like the devil," said he, "I'll go no further," and turned toward home.

— In the course of my sixth year Mr. Parker began making preparations for building a new house. One morning Dave and myself started early for the team, for the purpose of drawing two loads of lumber from Andover. All being found except one horse, I drove them home while Dave searched for the missing horse. Seeing one horse gone and Dave too, Mr. Parker cried out in his accustomed hoarse, angry tone, "Where is the horse? Where is Dave? Go and find Dave. Go get the horse. Go bait the oxen. Why don't you run?"

"I don't know what you mean," said I, "I never saw a man act as you do in my life."

Having the cart-whip in his hand he gave me a heavy cut around my legs, the knot in the end of the lash coming inside the knee hurt me considerably.

We started off together toward the pasture.

"Why don't you run," said he.

"If I go as fast as you do it is fast enough, I shall go no faster," said I. So we walked on silently together.

The next morning found the whip chopped into inch pieces, beside the hog-sty.

"Who did that?" said Parker.

"I did it," said I, "it was my own whip, and shall not keep a whip to whip myself with."

This was the first and only time he ever struck me while I lived with him. His course was decidedly a grief to Mrs. Parker, but it was out of her power to prevent it.

In haying time, that well known time of hurry and bustle, as we came home late for dinner one day, we found the women had eaten and nothing remained but some boiled indian pudding and five ears of boiled corn. There were more ears of green corn in the pot boiling. We soon cleared away the pudding, and Mr. Parker taking three ears and Raynor two, started for the further barn to throw off a load of hay, saying to me,

"Come along and take away that hay."

"Let him stop till the corn is done," said Mrs. Parker.

"No come right along now," said he, and on he pushed, eating as he went, which was his common practice.

I soon took two ears of hot corn alternating them from hand to hand and run after Raynor and overtook him gnawing his corn, and ran ahead. Mr. Parker called out from the yard,

"Get quick up on to the mow and take away the hay."

I scrambled up, as the corn was getting just cool enough to eat.

"Lay down your corn," said he, "if you can't eat your dinner while I eat mine and feed the hogs, you may go without. You thought because that lazy curse," meaning Raynor, "stayed behind you might."

I laid the corn on the plate under the eaves and it lays there now for aught I know. "I will have what I want to eat for time to come," said I, "and if you will not let me have it, I will go where I can get it."

"Where will you go?" said he.

"I will go to Ohio," said I, "before I will live with you another year, if you don't treat me better."

"What is that you say?" said he. It was repeated.

"Come right down to me and I will whip you for that."

I was on the load by him as soon as my weight would

fetch me there. He seized my arm and taking an alder stick from the hay, said, "Shall I strike you or not?"

"Just as you have a mind to," said I.

"Will you ever say it again?"

"I can't help thinking so, and I may as well say it as think it."

"If you do think it, you shan't say it in my hearing." Here he stuck the pitchfork into the mow and I clambered on to the top again, and Raynor who had listened to the whole came forward to help me. If he had struck me, it was my determination to slip off the hind end of the load and never work for him again.

"Come right down to me and I will whip you for that."

I was on the load by him as soon as my weight would fetch me there. He seized my arm and taking an alder stick from the hay, said,

"Shall I strike you or not?"

"Just as you have a mind to," said I.

"Will you ever say it again?"

"I can't help thinking so, and I may as well say it as think it."

"If you do think it, you shan't say it in my hearing." Here he stuck the pitchfork into the mow and I clambered on to the top again, and Raynor who had listened to the whole came forward to help me. If he had struck me, it was my determination to slip off the hind end of the load and never work for him again.

The writer would fain hope that few men, who have the care of youth, manifest so much indifference to their comfort as not to allow them time to well masticate their food.

A word here on diet. In the summer season, brown bread and milk was the constant food, for the whole family, morning and night. By brown bread is meant, bread made of rye and indian meal raised and baked in large loaves and in a brick oven, in those days. Supper for Saturday was uniformly roast potatoes and salt; no butter was used. The winter rations were beef-broth, with brown bread crumbled in, and for change, bean porridge. This porridge was made by boiling a piece of pork, with a handful of beans, till they had become soft and smashed, then dipped into dishes with bread crumbled in.

Our Sunday dinner was invariably baked beans with salt pork, and a baked indian pudding. A little butter was allowed for the pudding.

Thanksgiving festival was indeed a luxury. We commonly had fowls and roasted pork, or spare-rib, and plum puddings, with as many as three kinds of pies, — mince, apple and pumpkin. We had as nice a treat at Thanksgiving then, as they scare up now, and ate it with a greater zest.

It should be remembered that the time of which I have been speaking was more than half a century ago. Great changes have since taken place, as might be expected, both in food and dress.

My clothes in summer were — straw hat, tow shirt and tow trowsers. When the mornings were cool, I put on my vest such as it was, and my frock if required. I had no shoes until the ground began to freeze.

Winter habiliments were — striped blue and white woollen trowsers, fulled cloth vest and jacket. They were commonly made of Parker's or Dave's old ones, which good mother Parker took care to have well mended, much to my comfort. I was never allowed an overcoat while I lived there, or a pair of boots. I was allowed but one pair of shoes for two years. Parker used to tell me, when going to get my foot measured, to put on two pair of stockings, and tell the shoemaker to be sure and make them large enough to last two years.

The first year I put old flannel, or baize as it was then called, around my feet to keep the shoes from slipping and wearing out my stockings. When they needed repairs, Mr. Parker would, as he kept shoemaking tools on hand, tap them with old upper stuff and fill them full of nails to make them last well; and mother Parker would make me leggings from his old stocking legs.

At length Mr. Parker's father passed off the stage; the new house was finished; Dave was married and moved into it, but Raynor lived with us still. Now the battle raged wilder and hotter between Parker and Raynor, till at length they needed no interpreter, but were ready on all occasions to vociferate hard words at each other.

Catching a wild goose by hands must be considered noteworthy. One day as Raynor and myself were going to our labor we espied two wild geese in a little pond near by. We went toward the pond wanting to catch them, but hardly expecting such an event, as we had no firearms. Away they flew and we stood gazing after them. They soon wheeled and came back, but did not drop fast enough to hit the water, but passed over and alighted in thick bushes close beside where we stood, each secreted behind a tree. As they could not arise for entanglement, we sprang upon them simultaneously, each catching one by the neck and saving it. We tied their legs with some string which we had in our pockets, when luckily a man named Angier came along and took them to his house near by for safe keeping, Raynor paying him 50 cents for doing it. At night we laid them upon hay on the top of our load of wood and carried them home and put them in a pen in the hophouse. From discontent, or some other cause, not one mouthful would they eat, and we were obliged to cram them with corn to keep them alive. However, Raynor soon sold them to a man in South Reading for $5.

The year the new house was built, all was hurry and drive,— every nerve must be strained for labor. For instance, Parker would carry feed to his hogs with part of his dinner in his hand. He made calculation to start for work with as much in his hands as he could dispose of before he reached the field. A neighbor, whose field he often crossed, smilingly observed, "I must prosecute Parker for throwing his bones into my grass."

To accelerate business and encourage me, Mr. Parker said, that if I would keep the hops, corn, and potatoes well tended, after the first hoeing, all the season, he would give me twenty-five lbs. of hops, and I should have the steers to help me, and might plow as well as I pleased. The steers were a fine pair, three years old, of my own training, and were ox-handy.

One day, in Parker's absence, as I was plowing the potato patch both ways, Dave observed me, and halloing forbade the cross-plowing. As I paid no attention to what he said, he ran toward the field, which was in island form, then surrounded by mud. He had been unwell, and on that account wore stockings and shoes. While divesting his feet of their incumbrance in order to plunge through the mud, I hastened the steers at a rapid rate, plowing only one furrow in a row. Of course he took the team away from me, which greatly impeded that day's work. On Mr. Parker's return he discountenanced Dave's proceedings, and said he should help me as much as he had hindered. I told him my determination to hoe every hill myself. On examination he greatly approved my plan of cross-plowing, as the ground was of a clammy nature; indeed the crops bore unmistakable testimony to the utility of the procedure.

Seven acres of corn, potatoes, and hops were planted and hoed twice that season solely by me and the steers. Many times, in the gray dawn of the morning, we might be seen in the field at work, to evade the heat of the day. This practice of early rising, in hot weather especially, I wish to recommend as the secret of realizing a good day's work.

FOURTH LINK

Hop picking came on, that season of hilarity in which boys and girls all participate. We were stripping them off full of glee, not one reaching out his hand in vain. Mr. Parker rode to Wilmington to inquire the prospects of the hop market, and on his return said Col. Blanchard offered him 25 cents per lb.

"Why didn't you take it," said I.

"Will you take that for yours?"

"Yes."

The money was counted out straightway, which was more than I had ever been the owner of before. This was done at the hop bin. He cheerily said, "now we shall see which has the best luck selling hops, you or I." He kept his till the following Spring, in hope of obtaining a higher price, and then sold them for 11 cents per lb. Such I have often observed to be the case when a fair price is refused.

Mr. Parker's extreme fretfulness may be seen in the following story.

It was mid-winter, and new snow had fallen to a considerable depth. In the morning he said, "When you have fed the cattle, go to shoveling paths." I did shovel all the paths we usually shoveled after a snow storm. I then inquired where he was. The women said he had gone in the direction of the watering place, about half a mile distant. I followed, and when I came up with him, he said, "Why didn't you come along to shoveling here?"

"I didn't know there was anything to be done here; we never shoveled here before."

"You might know the snow would drift in here, now the trees are cut away," said he.

After a few minutes' work, he said, "Go let out the cattle, and drive them down to drink; start on the cows first."

I knew this order to be wrong, but it was implicitly obeyed, and when they came into deep snow, the oxen pressed on to the annoyance of the cows, which made him exclaim, in wrath, "run ahead and stop that ox."

I had just exchanged my whip for his shovel, so I ran, shovel in hand, and called "whoa" to the ox, who was wont to stop at my bidding.

"What do you say 'whoa' to that ox for?" was his tart response.

"What a plague; can I say anything but 'whoa' to an ox when I want to stop him?"

"You shan't say 'plague' to me," said he, and ran at me with all his might, whip in hand.

I could not make much headway for the deep snow, and so turning round said, "Don't break the whip-stick; I paid eleven cents for it;" when he desisted.

Before we reached the house he met a neighbor, to whom he said, "Asa cares more for his whip than for his back, for when I was going to strike him, he said, 'Don't break the whip,' and I could not help laughing."

It was my aim, when he was in a pet, to make him laugh, if he had not got beyond the bounds of forbearance.

This Spring, Raynor left and hired out to a man who tilled the farm lying between Mr. Parker's two farms. I was commanded not to speak to him, which command I did not fully obey, as I was a staunch American, and unwilling to give up the right of free speech. Dave and his father still worked together.

Now as Dave and Raynor were gone, I was left alone to stand all the shots,— rifle, canister, grape and shell; and they fell thick and fast. Sometimes I thought it impossible to stay longer with him. But good mother Parker's sympathy and kind words did much to soften and heal the wounds, and I would conclude to await another broadside.

Soon after Raynor left, a traveller came along, and Dave took him in. He was a man of middle age. We never knew where he came from; if asked the question, he would not answer, but change the topic of conversation. He was no epicure, but would eat whatever was set before him. He slept in an attic chamber, with his door fastened. He was deranged in mind, and like other maniacs, when most crazy, would manifest a terrible temper. His name was Jeremiah Powers, and he could do a great amount of work, such as forking manure, hoeing, pitching hay, grain, &c; in doing any of these things, no man could beat him. He was exceedingly withy and spry. I have seen him stand with both feet together, and jump twelve feet ahead at a leap. Few men can do that.

In his worst spells, he would receive no directions about the work from any one except me, and would frequently urge me to join him to kill Parker and Dave, for he had a lunatic idea that if they were killed we could do as we pleased with the farm and stock.

Once on going into Dave's house, I found him sitting on a block in the corner, pale with terror, while Powers was standing over him, axe in hand, telling him if he moved he would split his brains out. And I believe he would have done so.

"Captain," said I, for we were used to calling him by that title, "what are you going to do with Dave?"

"Kill this old d—d regular," said he, "and take off his scalp."

"What are you going to do with it?"

"Sell it," said he.

"You can't get one cent for it; besides we want him to help get our hay in; he is good mower you know."

He turned away with a demoniac laugh, and Dave was relieved from his terror-stricken embarrassment. I must

confess I was frightened myself, but I made shift not to let
Powers know it. "Asa," said he, "you are always right; I will
let him go now."

He had a notion if any one hawked or spit, &c., they were
mocking him. If a cock crowed within his reach, he would
cut his head off if he could. Often while we were hoeing, the
fowls would come round picking up worms, and he killed
several in that way, when I would carry them into the
house and have them cooked. As he was one day pitching
hay, the horse, which was tied by a rope at the door, snuf-
fed. Powers told her if she did it again he would let her guts
out. The snuffing was immediately repeated, when Powers
sprang to the ground, pitchfork in hand. I screamed out,
"don't kill her, we want her to go fishing with, we can't go
on foot." He stopped short, saying, "You are always right; I
will let her live."

Another time he insisted that we must have our stints.
Accordingly Parker gave us a certain amount of plowing
and hoeing for that and the following day. The plowing was
done in the afternoon, which was followed by a bright,
moonlight night. Powers hoed alone all night, and the
morning found the work completed. "Now," said he, "you
are my man today; you shall do nothing for anybody else."
He soon decided to go fishing. We had two hooks, and I
bated them with angleworms while he fished. It was a day
of great sport to him, and I enjoyed seeing his cup of happiness so full. We carried home a mess of fish to cook.

Powers was uniformly good to me, but in no wise would I
suffer a son of mine to work with such an unfortunate. I
believe it may always be found true, that lunatics have
some one to doat upon. It is unquestionably better for them
to be constantly employed in outdoor labor; still they should
be carefully watched, for there is no telling the moment
when they may commit depredations.

Parker grew more and more unreasonable, but mother
Parker's faculty of smoothing over things seemed to increase.

Raynor's wife and children lived in our family, and he came home at night, which enraged Parker, especially if he found we spoke together. One morning as I entered the house with a handful of wood, I met Raynor at the door; we stopped and spoke. As Parker was coming out, he no doubt heard it. We soon went to unloading wood at the door; he was full of spite and many angry words found utterance. I told him at length I would leave him. He then caught a sled-stake and ran at me, but being smarter than he I ran out of his way. Mother Parker from the window, seeing him seize the stake, was struck with consternation lest he would injure me. However I stopped at speaking distance, and he told me to go to cutting brush, and said I should not drive the team any more, he would drive it himself. This was done with a view to plague me, because I loved teaming wo sell.

I did ot go to cutting brush as he said, but walked over to Dave's musing as I went on what I had best do. I told him my purpose of going away. He said, "you had better go to cutting fagots," which I did.

I would here say, my operation of cutting fagots, to procure a little pocket money, proved a rod for my own back. All my spare hours, rainy days, &c., were necessarily filled up with fagot making. The last three months I lived with him, I carried home to him $72 taken for fagots, all of my own making.

I soon stopped my work and returned to the house. I told Mrs. Parker I was going to leave. She wept and said, "No, you must not go, I will try and get him to treat you better."

"It is of no use," said I. "I have tried that long enough. I don't want to stay here to have my brains beat out."

"I do not blame you," said she, "but had rather you would not take your clothes. You shall eventually have them, but as he said you should not take them, I had rather you would not take them now."

"Good-bye,"—"good-bye,"—was alternated, and I was off on the road toward my own mother's.

I should have mentioned in connection with Parker's threatening with a sled-stake, that when I told him I would go away he said, "you cannot go; you are bound to me, and can't get away."

"No," said I, "not so. I have been informed that, as father, who bound me here, is dead, you cannot hold me now I am fifteen."

"Who told you that," said he. I did not answer that question. He had evidently been more tyrannical since I was bound.

This story shows what a prominent part a woman can take in smoothing her rough-hewn husband's path. A good wife like a good missionary, is self-sacrificing, always intent on the welfare of others.

Not more than three days had elapsed before Parker came to mother's for me to go back, stop a few weeks and then tell people that we had come to an agreement to dissolve, saying that then I should have my clothes and my sheep. He was good-natured, for he had been to a lawyer and found he could not hold me, as I said.

I was then fifteen years and five months old. I went back with him and whenever an opportunity offered he would urge me to agree to stay three years with him; promising to find all my clothes, let me go to school one month each winter, and at the expiration of the time to give me $200.

"No," said I, "I will agree to stop only on this condition, that I will go any time I wish, and you shall pay me accordingly." To this he agreed and mother Parker witnessed the contract. I felt then it was as safe as if put in black and white, and a justice had signed the acknowledgment. This occurred in the spring of 1804, and we set about raising eight calves, to pay my wages when the three years were out, as Parker said. Soon, however, his accustomed fretfulness got hold of him with renewed vigor and he disdained to give explicit orders, but wanted explicit compliance with all his desires.

Our State Election, that holiday for boys, when they

generally had two days given them for their pleasure, occurred on the last Wednesday in May. As I had but half a
day, I chose to take the last half of the second day.

After putting the cows in pasture, mother said, "Asa, I
wish you would hoe in the garden for me this morning." I
complied. When Mr. Parker came from the field his anger
could not be restrained because I had not been in the field
at work. "Eat your breakfast in one minute," said he. I
swallowed the bread and milk unceremoniously, till the
minute was out, and then set the bowl down. Mother then
brought her foot to the floor in her expressive manner,
saying, "Eat your breakfast, if you can't have time to eat
your breakfast Election morning I will leave the house." So
I finished it.

I should have stated before that our State Elections in
Massachusetts were held as festivals from time im-
memorial. At Mr. Parker's we always dined on roasted veal
and plenty of raised sweet cake, called Election cake. Elections, like Thanksgivings, were days much calculated upon.

To my story again. We worked along as well as could be
expected, "bearing and forbearing," till July, when it was
found out the calves were lousey and must be washed in
tobacco wash to cleanse them. Toward night I arranged to
drive them up, but it was foggy and they hid in the bushes
and vainly did I try to collect them. Returning, I found all
in bed, ate my spoon-victuals and retired. Early the following morning, the bushes wet as rain, I was out in search of
them, in hopes to get them home before Parker was up, but
failed in that endeavor. He was fiendish, cross and surly, I
saw at once. "Eat your breakfast," said he, and wash the
calves, by the time I get mine done."

My bowl of breakfast was soon dispatched, and one calf
was finished ere he came out.

"Turn out the calves," said he, "and go right to mowing."

"Why, that would be a pity," said I, "as the wash is all
ready and they are here."

"Then do it quick," said he, "if you do it at all."

The eight calves were quickly and faithfully washed, and when they were turned into the street to be driven to pasture, he cried out,

"Let the calves alone, let them go where they please, and you shall pay for them if they are lost."

"It will take but a few moments and it is a pity to have them stray away," said I. The calves were put in the pasture and I hastened to the mow-field where he was mowing, but found him cross as a bear. The grass was furze and hard to cut; soon he stopped to whet his scythe, and when done, reached out his hand for mine. I gave it. "Why don't you take my scythe and mow in my swath while I when yours," said he.

"Because it is as much as I can do to keep up with you, as fast as you mow this morning." This was my first year of mowing, and I was not 16 years old.

"You lazy dog, you have not earned your salt this fortnight," grated in my ears.

"'Tis a new thing to be called lazy," said I, "and if I have not earned my salt, you shall not find it any longer. I shall leave at once, and would like to have you pay me for the time I have worked for you, according to agreement."

"No," said he, "you will probably choose a guardian and I will settle with him. You may take your clothes."

When at a little distance he called saying, "you shan't have your clothes." I proceeded to the house, sat down on the doorsill, talked with Mrs. Parker, and heartily wished, as I had many times before, that circumstances were such that I could consistently stay; as at that time it was deemed disreputable for a boy to change places often. And besides I had no expectation of getting so high wages any where else, being only 15 years and 9 months of age, having lived with him 7 years, 8 months, and 10 days. Tears fell. Soon Parker came and seeing me, said, "If you are going to go, go — I don't want you sitting on my doorsill." I was off.

The next day the man who owned the farm that lay between Mr. Parker's two, seeing me, offered me good wages to work for him, if Parker would not be mad about it. "You had better go and see him," said I. He went. Parker said he did not want me to be idle, and I might as well work for him as anybody.

The next Saturday afternoon as Parker crossed our field he said, "If you will bring them back at night, you may have your clothes to go to meeting tomorrow." The offer was accepted, and the clothes returned according to order.

Thus things continued, always taking my clothes back to Parker's every Sabbath night and locking them up, till my three months' engagement to Mr. Stone was out. Parker then gave me my clothes,— the sheep I had previously sold, — but would not pay the money. His excuse was, that it was a damage to him to have me go away, as he could not get as much labor done so cheaply in any other way, and so he would not pay it.

I did not consider it best to commence a prosecution for so small a sum as $20. It is an old maxim, notwithstanding a good one, "Keep out of the law."

Subsequently, consulting Capt. Daniel King, of Danvers, in respect to being my guardian, he said, "you can take care of yourself; I will give you such advice as you may need, and when you have any money to spare, bring it to me, I will keep it for you, and that will do as well as a legalized guardian." I followed his directions, and from time to time put small sums of money into his hands.

FIFTH LINK

You next find me in a gentleman's family in Salem, as their waiting man, at $12 per month. The gentleman was sick up stairs, but his wife was one of the *unsufferables*. She never allowed her maid to enter the dining room where she and her son took their meals.

I laid the table and cleared it again, and waited on them while eating. The last thing set on the table was a bell beside her plate. When eating, I must sit in the adjoining room near the door, to await the ringing of the bell.

"Ting, ting, ting; bring a bottle of wine from the cupboard." Done, and I just seated.

"Ting, ting, ding," again; "pour out a glass of wine for me." Done.

"Ting, ting-a-ling ding; pour out a glass for Edward." Done.

"Ting, ting, ting," again; "fill up Edward's glass full."

And so it was from morn till night. It seemed to be her steadfast plan to keep me always running; and in order to fulfill her purpose, she would not suffer me to bring more than one thing at a time, when it could be done just as well as not. For instance: She wanted a half-peck of rye meal, and sent me three-fourths of a mile to buy it. When done she asked the price and gave me the change all to one cent. "It wants one cent more," said I, "that piece will go for only five cents."

"Do you think I don't know money," said she.

"Yes, and so do I too."

The money was carried, when the man observed, "There is one cent lacking, but no matter."

"What did the man say to the money," said she, when I returned.

"He said, 'it lacked one cent, but no matter.'"

"Here, go carry the cent; I will owe nobody."

So here was three times the travel necessary, and more too, for there was plenty of rye meal for sale, of the same quality, the next door to hers.

These people had a garden of vegetables near Beverly Bridge one mile from home. She one day sent me for three kinds of vegetables, telling me to go three times; and also which to bring first, which second, and which last. I had learned a little about favoring myself, and brought them all at once, leaving two kinds with a wood-sawyer I was acquainted with, while I carried one kind home. I then returned, stopped awhile, and carried another kind home, and lastly the other kind. This was satisfactory, because it was not known but that I went to the garden for the three kinds at different times.

This kind of treatment too, was far from agreeable; I hardly expected to like it when I commenced. The man appeared well, as far as he appeared at all; but that heartless woman, oh! that heartless woman! how many times I wished that she might become poor, and be obliged to wait on herself. She did die poor.

I gave notice that I must leave in three weeks from commencing. The man urged me to stay, but I was decided.

"If you cannot be contented here," said the woman, "you would not be in heaven."

"That depends on the company," said I, and cleared for deeper water.

After the gentleman's recovery he made an attempt to hire me again into his family. I told him the work did not suit me, and besides I would not live with his wife at any price. I would rather dig ditches for a living than work for her.

I now steered back to my old neighborhood in North Reading, and let myself to Parson Stone through haying and harvesting, and worked for board in the winter and attended school.

On vacant school days, I sometimes would drive a load of wood to Salem for the Parson, for 25 cents. I well remember buying cotton cloth for shirts for myself, at 30 cents per yard, — five cents more for one yard than I had for a day's work; and it was called very cheap, much cheaper than it had been. This should put those to the blush who now complain of the present prices, which are not half so high.

I used to think at that time if there was as much difference between heaven and hell as between Mr. Parker's and Parson Stone's, there was difference enough.

It was my good fortune, through the influence of Capt. king, my adviser, to hire out to bachelor Jonathan King of Danvers. A niece of his kept his house. They were good people to live with, and had one other hired hand named Clark.

Clark was a man of intemperate habits, and when half drunk was bad to get along with. Once when plowing, because he could not keep the plow in the furrow, he insisted on driving the cattle, but made out no better. He shifted the oxen from nigh to off, and off to nigh sides alternately, but to no purpose, and forced the steers so hard they split the yoke. King being informed of the case by his niece, said, "Asa, you had bad work with the steers, did you?"

"I was not teamster today, sir."

"Did I not give you the care of the team?"

"Yes, sir, but a stronger man than I took it from me."

"Well, you take charge of the team now, and never give it up for any one."

I drove it ever afterwards while I lived with him.

I will here mention a narrow escape which I had, the effect of inebriation. A little party of us went out in a boat fishing. Toward night a fog arose that wholly obscured the horizon, and when it came time to row homeward, all but me were turned round and were for going out to sea. I told them the opposite direction was homeward, but they would not believe me. They had carried New England rum with them, of which all drank but me. Clark, not a little tipsy, caught me up and would have thrown me overboard had not a friend seized him, and with assistance threw him down on the bottom of the boat and held him there. We then rowed on with all our might, and when some became disheartened I told them if we did not hear a rapping on the ship that was building at the shore within half an hour, I would give up my say. In less than twenty minutes we heard the taps, and soon gained the shore in safety.

Beware, oh! beware, of intemperate companions, but more especially beware of the intoxicating cup. Too much caution cannot be used in the selection of associates. They should be none but those of thorough-going temperance principles. The young are little aware of the influence of companionships to lead insensibly to vice of any and every kind. Strong drink, as a beverage, should be held in perfect abhorrence. "Touch not, taste not, handle not," is the only safe ground to stand upon.

My time being expired at King's, I was hired by Jesse Upton of North Danvers, tavern-keeper, for $13 per month for one year.

King hired another hand in my stead, who was unwilling to work with Clark, still he was preferred and Clark paid off. Clark came to Upton's to get me to persuade him to hire him, which I refused on account of his love of strong drink.

Mr. Upton had been a prosperous man in life, and had now married a second wife, who I thought very complete and handsome. The men would reply to me, with a significant shake of the head, when I spoke of her, "You do not know her." Light on that subject soon began to develop, when one day we hesitated about starting off to Salem with wood, fearing rain. On my observing that I would venture myself if he would the team, it was concluded to go. Rain soon began to fall, and increased to a gale before I reached home at 5 o'clock in the afternoon. Four carriages drove into the yard for shelter at the same time that I did, although not far from their homes. Mrs. Upton called from the house, "Asa, let your team stand, and unharness and take care of those horses." Not having eaten a mouthful since breakfast, and being completely drenched with rain, I obeyed the summons, sheltered my team, and made shift to get on dry clothes as soon as possible. Immediately two other carriages drove up, whom Hutchinson, the waiting man, proceeded to wait upon. Mrs. Upton seeing this, told him to call me to unharness. There were six men in the barn husking corn, and I had joined them, and when he gave me the order I told him the horses might stand there, for I should not expose myself again to rain that night.

So much tavern company to eat first, made it past 7 o'clock, before I had a mouthful to eat. She informed Mr. Upton in my hearing of these facts, when he said, "Asa, you did wrong in one thing, you ought not to have unharnessed the horses."

One circumstance will serve to show the care practised at that early time in life to secrete money. I was sent, in company with another hand, to Charlestown with two loads of hay. I took the pay for both loads, it was in bills, and amounted to $100. There had recently been a robbery perpetrated in Lynn Woods, through which we passed. On our way home, I must say that I felt a little anxiety on that account and kept a sharp lookout. Observing a man coming up to the hind team, I took the money from my pocket and put it in the near ox's ear and stopped the team, standing close beside him. The man came up, and proved to be a neighbor there, exchanged a few words of civility and passed on. I then took the money from its safe depository, saying to the hand that, "I had stopped to let the oxen breathe," and started on.

Being 17 years of age, I was entrusted by Mr. Upton to go on monetary business from town to town, with orders to put up for the night, if I pleased, much to his apparent satisfaction.

He left home one day, giving me orders to meet him in Boston with a load of hay, and to bring fifteen kegs of pickles. I brought the kegs from the cellar and asked Hutchinson to hand them up to me to place on the load. Just then Mrs. Upton said,

"Can't you load those pickles alone?"

"Not very well," said I.

"Then you need not carry them;" and the pickles were not taken.

I then opened my provision box, saw nothing there that I could eat, and left it and started. I drove all day and all night; ate but little; reached home between daylight and sunrise; fed the team, and turned into bed.

The next day said Mrs. Upton, "Mr. Upton, if our hired men can't eat as we do, when they go on the road, I think it is fine times."

"Where is that box of provision?" said Mr. Upton, "call Betty."

"Where is the box of provision put up for Sheldon, Betty, bring it here?"

"I can't do it," said she, "I threw it into the hog-pail; it was not fit for anybody to eat."

"Mrs. Upton how much do your men usually spend on a day's teaming; if I have spent more I will pay it back."

"I do not know how much they spend," said she, "but I know how much they ought to spend."

She then took a slate and carefully marked down what the reasonable expenses of a day would be, allowing 25 cents for dinner, &c., and the amount swelled to 20 cents more than I laid out. Upton, who was a whole-souled man, pulled out his purse quickly, and handed me the 20 cents saying, "I will pay that if I never have another cent."

The following story will serve to show how the faithful are regarded by their employers, and also how a vixen of a wife can mar and blast the happiness and prosperity of her husband.

Business called Mr. Upton away to be gone several weeks. He directed me to take the team to Londonderry and buy and bring home two barrels of sour cider for vinegar making. I was to carry up a load of household goods from Salem. It was in the month of April, the distance was 50 miles, and road new to me and muddy. Nothing noteworthy occurred until I reached Derry and came to a tremendous hill, as it then appeared to me. I stopped at its base and fed the cattle; while they were eating I walked up the hill to see what the prospect was of getting up alone. A couple of boys were plowing with four oxen near by. I inquired if they would help me up the hill. They said the team belonged to Gen. Reed. I must go and ask him, he lived ahead. I went.

"Can't your team take the load up," said he.

"Yes," said I, "but I do not want to put them to the utmost of their power."

"You may take them," said he, "for I see you are careful of your cattle."

I took them along as far as I wished. When against his house, I stopped the team and he came out with a white mug of cider.

"Have you cider to sell," said I.

"Yes, come down into my cellar and see."

I went and beheld 200 barrels in one cellar, the greatest amount I ever saw, before or since. I soon agreed with him for 10 barrels at $2 per barrel, with the barrels, they being new. I went and unloaded the goods and returned and stopped over night with the General, the next day I set forward, and had a prosperous journey home. I was only 17 years, 6 months old. Sold one barrel in North Reading on my way home for $4, a nice profit.

Shortly after, with Mrs. Upton's consent, I took the team and went again for 10 barrels more of cider, for which I had previously agreed, if I wished to come for it.

At this time the old General observed, "I see you are very careful of your team, and very cautious too in buying for your employer, and I should like to hire you to live with me."

"I am engaged for a year," said I.

"Then," said he, "if you ever come this way, I should like to have you call and see me." A few years afterwards I heard of his death.

On reading home I found that Mrs. Upton had hired two men, — one large man for $11 per month, and another small one for $10 per month.

"Asa," said she, "how much do you have per month?"

I replied, "$13."

"Oh, fie, I can hire men big enough to eat you up at two meals, for $11; so I will pay you off."

I took the money and repaired immediately to good old Parson Stone's. Soon after Mr. Upton came, and to induce me to return, offered $15 per month for a year.

"I would not live with your wife at any price," was the decided answer.

A narrow escape occurred while living with Parson Stone, which gratitude forbids I should omit; showing the benefit of bleeding after a fall. Edward Stone and myself were threshing rye in the barn. I went on to the high scaffold for purpose of throwing down the bundles; they were piled up near to the ridgepole. While standing on one bundle the band gave way and I found myself sliding rapidly down, and must be precipitated to the barn floor. In falling I called to Edd to catch me, but a glance showed him running away. It is certainly astonishing how swiftly thoughts will run at such a moment as this. I thought if he would just catch hold of a shoulder or any other part it would ease the fall, and I felt sorry to see him run away. As

I slid from the broken bundle I came feet foremost; but in the descent, as kind Providence ordered, one foot touched the edge of the scaffold and tipped me broadside, thus breaking the force of the fall, and I came plump on my side upon the barn floor, my head resting on a flat stone used for laying on a corner of the winnowing sheet. I jumped up feeling no pain, sprang to the barn door and fell. My eyesight left me, which caused an alarm that I should never see again. Edd took me on his shoulder and conveyed me to the house.

"What is the matter with Asa?" said the Parson.

"He fell from the top of the rye to the barn floor," said Edd.

"Carry him in and take care of him, and I will go for the doctor."

When he arrived, he bled me in the arm, and as soon as the blood touched the bowl my sight returned. The first object that greeted my joyful eyes was good Madam Stone holding the bowl. All the while I had sense enough to know what was going on, but could neither see nor speak.

SIXTH LINK

I remained with Parson Stone till the death of his son in September, when, by his request, I was hired by his son's Administrator to take charge of affairs there, with orders to cut and carry to market wood enough to supply the family's wants and pay my wages. At first I boarded with the widow, till in a few months she married; then I boarded with his first wife's mother, and a better woman to take care of everything and everybody could not be found.

In April following, I let myself to Capt. Daniel Graves, Mr. Stone's farm being let and the personal property sold at auction. Here I had full charge of the farm concern, Mr. Graves' son working at brick-laying in Boston. If ever my ambition was raised, it was then. When the moon favored me with her light, my scythe was frequently running in the grass by 3 o'clock in the morning.

Capt. Graves' father, who was near 80 years of age, lived with him. When he hired me, he said he hoped I would try and please his father, for the hired hands were inclined to differ with him. I determined to keep the right side of him, if possible; so when a piece of work was to be done, I would say to him, "Hadn't we better do it in this way?" He almost invariably answered, "Yes;" and so well did I succeed in my attempt to please the good old gentleman, that the summer passed without a discordant word. Indeed, so interested did he become in all the concerns, and so much assistance did he afford, that I frequently pitied his fatigued state. The family were pleasant and kind, and I enjoyed life well this season.

In 1807, I was hired by Major Aaron Pearson, and came to Wilmington, where I soon made the acquaintance of Mr. Jabez Gowing's family. There I found congenial friends. I must say they seemed more like relatives than any other family known. Mr. Gowing's family name was Jaques, and like others of that name, was always able to impart information to every listener.

Mr. Pearson owned a saw mill in company with two others, and much of my business was lumbering, a kind of work that suited me.

When about twenty years of age, I bought the said saw mill in company with John Nelson. Nelson was anxious to build a grist mill, and as I refused to go him company in it, he set it up himself. At length finding himself in embarrassed circumstances he sold me the whole concern, both saw and grist mill. This was merely a winter mill, as no right was given to plow the land in summer. I vividly remember the grist mill was raised on the day I was 21.

Shortly after, on Nov. 13, 1809, at 25 minutes past 10 o'clock in the morning, by Nelson's watch, an event occurred which I shall never forget; for I shall carry indubitable proofs of it to my grave. While engaged in moving a loaded wagon, I fell under it, one wheel passing over my hat, and another over my left leg, not only breaking, but smashing it. Under the misguided judgment of the oldest man in the company, this sad affair took place. The bone was well set by Frank Kittridge of this town.

The fact that drinking alcoholic spirits was universally practised at this time, should be kept in mind. This custom will be better understood by reading the following poetry.

> How different some customs are,
> With mortals here below,
> From what they were when I was young,
> Some fifty years ago.

One could not have a 'raising' then,
Without a keg of rum,
'Twere of no use to ask the men,
For sure they would not come.

The Doctor would not ride a mile,
To save a man from dying,
Until he had a glass of sling,
And then he'd be for trying.

The Lawyer could not plead a case,
For plaintiff or defendant,
Until he took a glass of gin,
And then there'd be no end on't.

The Minister, he could not preach,
Extempore or by note,
Unless he had a glass of wine
To guzzle down his throat.

One could not go to market then,
However near or handy,
Without he had, to help along,
Some good old Cognac brandy.

One could not mourn e'en for a friend,
A friend however near,
Unless he had a cordial glass,
To prove himself sincere.

The Sailor couldn't sing a song,
The Yankee couldn't whittle,
With any kind of grace at all,
Unless he had a little.

— *Bard of Souhegan, Amherst, N.H.*

According to custom I prepared myself with liquor to treat all who favored me with their company, and many otherwise lonesome hours were beguiled with friendly chat.

A week or ten days after the accident, as Dr. Kittridge was dressing the wound, I raised myself upon my elbow and saw that he was cutting out a bit of flesh the size of a quarter of a dollar. "What are you doing, doctor?" said I. He then run in his probe, the marrow spouting up like water, and said, "does that hurt you?"

"No; if I did not see you, I should not know you touched it."

"O, I had rather heard you scream like murder," said he.

He then bound up the leg, went and sat down by the fire with elbows on his knees and buried his face in his hands for several minutes.

With sad countenance he approached the bed saying, "Asa, I must tell you one thing."

"Let me hear it," said I.

"You must have your leg cut off, or lose your life within forty-eight hours, because mortification has set in and it can't be stopped."

He then left, was absent about two hours, and returned with four other doctors, one being his father.

They examined the leg and said it had got so bad I could not live over thirty-six hours, unless it was amputated. I told them I would not have it taken off. If I died, I would die altogether. They paid no attention whatever to what I said, but went to work and spread out their instruments on the table. The sight of them struck me with horror indescribable. I felt as though they meant to dissect me.

"Mary," said I, "give me a little of that rum and molasses."

"Shall I, doctor?" said she.

"Give him a little," said the doctor.

"Shall I give him that," said she, showing the glass.

"Yes," said he, "that will not hurt him."

I drank it and said, "Frank, come here."

He came to my bedside, when I said, "No man shall cut my leg off while I have my senses. If I lose my senses and it is cut off, and I can find out who did it, I will shoot him, let him be who he may."

"You are good pluck," said he, "I'll cure you if I can."

I assure you that they put up their tools in "short meter," bound up the wound and all left but the old doctor, who like a faithful friend, as he was, stuck by me day and night. He

was an old gentleman and very lame; he could not walk a
step without crutches. He sat in an arm chair by the bed,
with two young women to wait upon him by turns, — six
hours each by rotation. His order to them was, if he was as-
leep to wake him every fifteen minutes, when he would
apply something to the wound. I often asked how the case
came on, but he always answered evasively. When the clock
struck at the end of thirty-six hours, he suddenly started in
his chair and said, "you've beat them. The thirty-six hours
are out and your leg is better than two wooden legs." He
staid two days longer, but did not dress the limb quite so often. From that time I never failed to give the old man a
quarter whenever I met him. He would say, "Hey! boy, you
remember that leg."

My mother, hearing of my misfortune and that it was expected I should lose my limb or my life, came to see me
with a view to stop and take care of me. I thanked her, but
said, "Mother, I do not want you; I had rather have the
prettiest girl I ever saw, than such a long face."

At the expiration of seventeen wearisome days and
nights, I was helped off my bed, but in less than ten
minutes I was glad to be helped back, where I lay seventeen days more, much against my will.

Being partially recovered, on Jan. 18, I rode horseback to
Danvers, where my brother Elbridge lived. I stopped with
him a short time and returned homeward to Capt.
Howard's, who married sister Lucinda. The day was very
unusually warm for winter, and I am sure I never saw
more cattle on the road, in one day, with their tongues out,
in my life.

The next morning brought a great change. It was the
memorable January 19th, 1810, or "Cold Friday." The cold
was intense. In several instances within my knowledge,
people perished. It was noted for half a century by almanac
makers. Since my remembrance, I have never known so
sudden a change as we experienced at this time, although

people are often saying, "The weather changes oftener than it used to."

In this connection a few observations on the weather may not be unimportant. You will find that these signs rarely fail.

If rain commences between daylight and sunrise, there will be but little rain. Start on your journey if you are inclined.

If rain commences between 12 and 1 o'clock, or at midday or midnight, there will be six hours of rain, more or less.

Where the wind is at sunset Candlemas day, or February 2d, there will be its home for two months. It will never be away from home more than forty-eight hours at a time. Should it be North or North-west, look out for cold weather.

Note the day the first snow falls and to that add the age of the moon the day that it falls, and the product will be the number of snows to come that year. For example, if the first now falls the tenth day of the month and the moon is fifteen days old, add ten to fifteen, and you have the number of snow storms for that year.

When a halo, or circle, around the moon is seen, if one bright star appears in the circle there will be one fair day and then rain. If two bright stars appear there will be two fair days and then rain. But if no stars are within the circle the following day will be rainy. There are more exceptions to this rule than any of the others.

If the sun cast a red reflection on the clouds in the morning, rain will follow that day.

If the sun cast a red reflection at night, any night in the week except Thursday, it will be fair the next day.

If the sun set in a cloud Thursday night, there will be rain within forty-eight hours.

In regard to the Candlemas sign, I would say, that I never, in fifty years, knew it to fail but once.

To farmers, I wish to say, that if the months of April and May are dry, and there follow three weeks of wet weather in June, first or last, you may reckon on a fair crop of English hay.

About forty years ago, passing by 'Squire Adams' hayfield in Medford, about the 10th of June, I saw several hands mowing, while he was spreading swaths. "'Squire," said I, "I hope that that hay will all rot before you can get it into the barn."

"What have I ever done to you, that you should wish such a wish on me," said he, wonderingly and laughingly.

Three weeks from that day, as I passed that way, I saw the same hands opening the same hay for the first time, and in fact it was rotten. "Well," said the 'Squire, "you have your wish, the hay is rotten and I am glad of it."

I must add, the hay was opened on to a fine crop of rowen, that had grown since mowing, and which would have greatly enhanced the value of the crop had he waited four weeks longer.

— Now to my story again. In the morning, cold as it was, I was determined to make the attempt to get home, in spite of the remonstrances of friends. Being well wrapped up and shielded from the cold, brother Howard brought me home in his chaise with my horse tied behind, and staid over night. Two men in Woburn went into a lot to chop wood that day, and both perished. Their death may partially be attributed to their having New England rum with them.

Another instance will suffice to show the intensity of the cold. A stage driver, seated on his box, was frozen stiff, with the reins for four horses clenched with a death grasp. The horses turned up to their accustomed hotel, when the driver retained his seat, much to the astonishment of the passengers, who were fastened in. The fact was soon developed, that the driver was frozen to death.

In sympathy with my misfortune, the citizens generally offered to give each a day's work, cutting or drawing lumber, if I would purchase it. Accordingly an acre of standing wood and timber was bought of Wm. Blanchard, Esq., for

$100. It was situated about forty rods west of Maj. Pearson's, my boarding place.

A day was set, and notice given that I would find a warm dinner, but they must bring forage for the teams.

I bought one barrel of cider; the butcher made a generous consideration on the beef, and on applying to Capt. Joseph Bond, the first, and extensively known, cracker baker in Wilmington, for bread, he magnanimously gave all the crackers wanted and several pans of gingerbread. Mrs. Pearson and her daughter Mary did the cooking gratis.

As many took their grub in the house as could be convened, others took theirs at the door by means of barrels covered with boards. They had plenty of roast beef, good boiled potatoes, crackers and cider. This last article was finished that night.

Some backed up their gift by coming the next day, when the lot was cleared and the logs drawn ashore, but not all drawn to the mill. On the first day there were 45 men and 20 yoke of oxen. Although lame, I procured a handy yoke of cattle and managed to draw the remaining logs to mill, about one and one-third miles, that winter.

SEVENTH LINK

The next spring, being unable to work on a farm, I let myself to brother Elbridge to drive a market cart, at low wages.

I next hired out to Capt. Stephen Abbott of Andover. When arranging the bargain, he said, "I want you to try if possible to please my father. If you cannot please him and me too, be sure and please him."

I thought better of him for that, and was certain he would be a good man to work for. To spurn the wishes of the aged, I am sorry to say, is too prevalent, but nevertheless indicates great lack of sensibility. Who are the party to be pleased, but the original owners? And I advise them never to give up their ownership as long as life lasts.

In looking back upon the summer spent in Mr. Abbott's family, I reckon it as one of the green spots in life; an oasis never to be forgotten. The old gentleman was so completely ingratiated into my favor, that nothing I did was amiss. Phebe, his daughter was a fine girl,—good in every sense of the word.

Capt. Stephen and wife were Christians, possessing "pure and undefiled religion," if we may be allowed to judge from the Scripture rule, "by their works ye shall know them."

It was customary in those days to buy cattle by the pound, to be weighed after dressing. I knew his integrity to be such that he would not cheat a man out of a pound in weight, or an ounce of tallow.

With regret I left that family in early winter, as my mill-pond had filled up and logs were in waiting. I took lodgings again at Major Pearson's and tended the mill. I stuck close and worked hard day and night. At one time, I kept the saw running five days and five nights all myself, excepting five hours. I then said that I would never work so hard again, even if it was to keep out of the poorhouse.

Spring opening, I set up butchering in company with James Dean, and boarded with him. I found, in this family, a similarity to Mr. Parker and his wife,—a woman amiable and gentle yoked with a tiger.

Times being dull, a new idea came up. I thought to take a two-horse load of groceries, and go back into the country to trade. I took tea, coffee, chocolate, tobacco and some rice. At Mt. Vernon traded a chest of tea for a fat cow; I left her to be sent to Dean's in Wilmington, in Flint's drove, and went on. I put up at Gibson's tavern, Francistown, over the Sabbath, and started early Monday, crossed Concord River at Windsor bridge, and soon saw the sign, "Allen Hayse." I offered a barter trade with him, when he handed me a piece of paper, saying "Put down every article and your price, and if I trade I shall pay in butter at 8 cents per pound."

When done, he said, "All but the rice I will take; you must take 75 cts. off that, and I will take the whole."

It was agreed upon, and the butter proving good, I started back the same night; carried the load to Salem and sold it for 12½ cts. per lb., making a good profit.

The cow was bought by friend Abbott, the butcher, before I reached home; he said he would give me $2 more than I gave for it, which allowed $1 profit and $1 for drift.

Another journey similar to that was made, with less profit, as butter had risen, making it uncertain business.

The next autumn, for the advantage of being nearer the mill, I boarded at Joshua Harnden's tavern, and attended to lumbering the next winter. My plan was to buy a woodlot, top and bottom; to hire the wood chopped by the cord, the lumber by the thousand, and to draw it into the mill myself, a man being hired to tend the mill.

Let me here tell a fox story. As I was returning from Salem, in company with Capt. Ezra Kendall, of Wilmington, and when between my mill and boarding house, we espied a fox run across the road. "Run," said I to Kendall, "and head him, and I will stand and give him a cut if he comes back on the same track." He did so.

"He is coming," said Kendall. I stood ready, keeping an eye on him. He looked back several times to make sure he was safe from his driver, but did not notice me, as he always turned his head the other way. When within reach of the whip, I gave him a cut and he fell to the ground with a scream, apparently dead. I took him up by the nape of the neck; he was limpsy as a rag, but as I carried him along he gave another childlike scream, with a desperate struggle, which so startled me that I came near dropping him. However, I held on till the house was gained, and gave him to two boys, who made a little pen of boards, covering it safely to prevent escape. During that night, foxes were heard about the house by the inmates, and when the morning came, lo! and behold, the boys were minus the fox. Other foxes had come in the night and dug him out, as evinced by the fact that the dirt from the burrow was thrown out on the outside.

To return to my narrative. About this time I was informed that David Foster, of Ashby, wished to sell a certain lot laying South of Thomas E. Upton's house. I made up my mind to start the next morning for the purpose of trying to buy it. That evening, coming across Capt. George Ford, he said to me, "Sheldon, do you want to buy a wood lot?"

"Yes," said I, "who has got one to sell?"

"I have; the Foster lot, front of Tom Upton's."

"What is your price?"

"$1500," was the answer.

"Will you take $1100."

"No, I have been offered $1300 for it today."

"Capt. Ford, do you own that lot?" said I, with not a little emphasis.

"Yes, I do, faith," said he.

As I looked him in the face, I discovered a blush. From that moment I made up my mind to carry out my first purpose.

Accordingly I made preparations to start for Ashby early the next morning. I told the landlady that I must start early and might not be home that night.

"Are you going to Salem?" said she.

"I do not know where I shall go, and if I am not back for two days you need not fear."

I was on my way as far as Westford before sunrise. Took dinner at Stone's Tavern, Townsend, left my horse and proceeded on foot to Mr. Foster's.

"Have you a woodlot in Wilmington to sell, Mr. Foster?"

"I have," he answered.

"What do you ask for it?"

"$1100," was the answer.

"Will you take $900?"

"No, I won't."

"What is the lowest you will take?"

"What pay can you make?"

"What pay do you want?"

"I want $300 down and the remainder in one year," said he.

"What security do you want for the $700?"

"Do you know Joshua Harnden?"

"I do; I board with him."

"Pay me $300 cash, and bring me a note for $700 with your name and Harnden's, and you shall have the lot."

"I want you to give me the refusal of that lot ten days, at the rate you have named, or for all the cash down," said I.

"Can you raise all the money," said he.

"If you will take $900 I think I can."

"I will not, but if you will bring me $930 you shall have it," said he.

I took out a ten dollar bill and presented it, saying, "if I do not come and comply with one of the above named terms within ten days, the bill is yours. If I do, it shall go toward the payment."

"If you don't have the land, I will have none of your money. My word is good for it," said he, "and that is enough."

I took a piece of chalk from my pocket and wrote both contracts on the ceiling over the fireplace, *verbatim*, thinking if it remained till I came again there would be hopes of getting the land. I considered it a great bargain.

Made the best of my way home, contriving a little circuitously to come up to the house from the way of Salem. The next day started for Henry Carter's store; I told him my business and asked what was the prospect for raising money to buy the Foster lot at $1100.

"Is it possible," said he, "that Ford would give you the refusal of that lot for $1100 when I offered him $1300?"

I told him, "Ford did not own it, the truth was I could have it for $930." Ford had had the refusal of the lot, but the time had expired. He had been written to on the subject, but took no notice of it.

The preliminary matters were arranged and I started with the $930 sewed into my vest pocket. Sure enough I felt a little chilly about the bargain, as Foster was a stranger and an illiterate man. On going into the house I saw that every letter of the chalk writing remained. My courage came back. Foster said, "I can't do anything with you today. But will give you $20 if you will do right. I felt doubtful and agitated, but said little. Soon he said, "Do you know Maj. D. Cummings of Andover?"

"Yes, I do."

"Well, he sent a hand up and offered $1000 for the lot, cash down, but I swear you have my word."

As nothing more could be done that day, I prepared to spend the night in this unique habitation. It had two rooms on the base, was one story in height, and unclapboarded. Two small glass windows in front and a board one in the rear that could be taken down at pleasure. A pretty good rough stone hearth, with a pine post near the fireplace, to support the garret floor. So much had been hewed off for kindlings that at the bottom it was not larger than a joist. Breakfast consisted of fresh pork steak well fried, roasted potatoes, doughnuts, and a cup of tea. In all it was good. And the curiosity was, Mrs. Foster had no other article to cook with but a dish-kettle. Everything cooked went through the dish-kettle, and they were considered wealthy. Before rising the next morning I heard the following conversation between Mr. Foster and a man whose farm he had bargained for.

"Has your man come up?" said the man.

"Yes, and I suppose he has got all the money, but I don't know."

"Then if he pays you the whole, I suppose you can pay me the whole," said the man.

"Yes if you will pay me for it," said Foster.

"How much must I give you?"

"Make your own offer."

"I'll give you $10."

"That will never do," was the response.

"I'll give you $15."

"That won't do neither."

"I'll tell you the most I will give, I'll give you $20."

"It's a bargain," said Foster. "Job, my son, run down to 'Squire Richardson's and tell him to come up and bring two deeds with him."

I was quick out of bed and dressed, and the reason was disclosed why he was not ready for me yesterday. The 'Squire was soon there. The deeds were executed, Foster signing them. His wife took up the pen to write but he held her back, and yet again, with the same effect. At length I threw a silver dollar on to the deed. "There, that will make the pen go," said Foster. And quickly the pen scratched her name.

"The clearing of this large lot of lumber was quite satisfactory. At the time War was declared in 1812, I had 200 cords of wood corded on the lot ready for market. In two days the price rose $2 per cord. I offered a string of forty-five cords to a man the day before the declaration, for $3 per cord. The day after the declaration, he came again and bought it for $5.

Mr. Ephraim Pratt, tanner, of North Reading, came into the lot and bargained for the bark on forty-five oak trees; he was to peel it himself and I was to team it, for $18. He wrote a contract with a pencil on a small bit of paper he chanced to have in his pocket, for all the bark on all the trees in the Foster lot, so called. I refused to sign it. He remarked, we know each other; we both know what it means. I then signed it. Mr. Pratt took with him to peel the bark, a man more trickish than he or I was. This man advised him to peel more than the forty-five trees as the contract was indefinite, and succeeded in persuading him to peel one hundred. On being applied to, to team off the bark, I refused, as there was no time set in the contract.

"What is the reason," said he, "that you will not team that bark?"

"You know as well as I do."

He then said, "How much shall I give you to team that bark and we be as good friends as we always have been?"

I said, "give me $18 more." He took the money out of his pocketbook and straightway gave it to me, saying, "Sheldon, I have felt worse about the peeling of that bark than you have. It is the first time I was ever persuaded by another man to do contrary to well understood agreement, and I am determined it shall be the last."

I was well acquainted with Pratt from his youth to his

death, and it is no more than justice to say, I considered him an upright, honest man, but for once he was induced to swerve by a sly, trickish man, who got no thanks from either party.

I will now state an event which took place at this time. My mother, then residing in Danvers, had a supposed claim on my old friend Joseph Tapley. However, they could not talk on the subject for irritation. "Mother," said I, "what is that claim worth?"

"It is worth $60, but I will sell it for $50, cash."

"I will give it," I answered. I went immediately to see Tapley, and told him I had bought mother's claim.

"Am glad of it," said he; "now I think we shall be able to settle it. Have you spoken with a lawyer?"

"No, I never spoke with a lawyer in my life," said I.

"Then we will go to Lawyer Putnam together."

He found the chaise and I the horse, and when we arrived there, he said, "Sheldon, you are the youngest, you may tell the story first."

I told the story as I understood it. Putnam then said, "Mr. Tapley, have you anything to say to this story, for or against."

"No, sir, it is as correct as I could state it myself."

"The claim is good," said Putnam, "and no man can better tell the worth of it, than you two. You both had better chalk what you think it worth."

We did chalk, and on examination found that Tapley had chalked $100, and I $120.

"Well," said Putnam, "that is as near as a buyer and seller could be expected to come. You had better split the difference."

This was speedily agreed upon. Putnam made out the documents for mother to sign. Tapley sold me a yoke of oxen for $60, and gave his note for $50. He then stated to Putnam that as we had come there for the amicable adjustment of our affairs, we had concluded to share the cost together, "Now what is your fee?"

"You love each other so well, and dislike quarrelling so bad," said Putnam, "that I will not take one cent. But this I must say, if everybody were of your minds, I would not give a mill for a lawyer's profession."

EIGHTH LINK

Capt. Joseph Bond had just given his business of baking into the hands of his sons Joseph and William. To increase their manufactures, they were at a loss how to procure fagots, which were then used exclusively for oven heating.

I told them there would be no trouble if they would pay enough for them. "It is such mean business, nobody will make them," they said.

"It will not be a mean business if you will pay a fair price for them."

"Who will make them, if we will pay well for it?"

"I will," said I.

"I should laugh to see you making fagots."

"I should laugh to see you paying me the money for it," said I.

The bargain was concluded between us, that I should make all I could in five days, anywhere in Wilmington where they could go with a team, and they would draw them and pay 1½ cents per bundle. At work I went, and in five days made 1000 bundles, for which they paid me $15. In less than a fortnight after, many respectable citizens, together with the minister, his two sons and the deacon, employed themselves in making fagots for the Bonds. And from that day to this it has never been considered mean business. Many a laboring man has earned a few dollars, who could not get it in any other way. Besides the benefit arising from the fagots themselves, it has been the cause of clearing many acres of swamp or low land, which proves the best land for cultivation we have in Wilmington.

In June, 1812, I commenced the business of carrying hops to Southern markets. I started with a two-horse team loaded with hops and shoes, for New York city, partly owned by myself and partly by others. This slow mode of transportation was resorted to, on account of the existing war. On arriving at New Haven, I found packets were safely running from there through Long Island Sound to New York and my hops could be carried for one-fourth cent per pound and my fare both ways thrown into the bargain. I thought best to take that course, and on my arrival found the brewers very ready to buy the hops which were soon disposed of, and last of all the box of shoes. The shoes were sold to a firm for $150. I procured a drayman to take them to the store. The storekeeper counted out the money, laid it on the counter, and then presented a receipt, which I signed and handed back to him. He took it, grabbing the money at the same time, exclaimed, "Now I have shaved the Yankee, I have the receipt, and you have not got the money."

I waited a few moments to see what he would do, as he had put the money away. Then I said, "will you pay me that money?"

He said, "I have your receipt for all I owed you."

"Did you hear that man say he had my receipt and I had not got my money?" said I to the drayman, whom I had designedly kept waiting.

"Yes," was his answer. As I stepped out of the store, I heard an elderly man say, "You have carried that joke too far with a stranger; you had better settle with him." Upon that he called me back, saying he would pay me. The difference between New York and Massachusetts money at that time, was 16 per cent. But it was understood that New York merchants in buying, expected to pay in New York money, as their banks had stopped specie payments. He then counted it out in New York bills. I said, "I can't take that, I must have Massachusetts money, or gold or silver, you have gone too far with me to have me accept that money."

"How much premium," said he, "shall I give on this money?"

"Sixteen per cent," said I. He straightway counted out the cash, $24. I pocketed the money; it was $24 more than I had expected; I then said, "if you have shaved the Yankee, you are welcome to the bristles," and then bade him "good-bye" with as much politeness as my Yankee blue frock would admit of. I then returned to New Haven, bought a load of flour at $8 per barrel, and started my team for home. At Worcester, I saw a company about to raise a signpost. I asked the man if he had opened a tavern. He said, "I am ready to." I then called for dinner for myself and horses. He asked if I would sell a barrel of flour, which I did for $18, and took pay in 18 bushels of buckwheat. His name was Charles Stearns. He said I was the first man who had patronized him. Nearly all the buckwheat sold for $3.50 per bushel, and the flour at $18 per barrel. The next morning, I started back to Worcester for another load of buckwheat. I succeeded in buying as before, at $1 per bushel, but when I returned wheat had fallen and I realized only a fair profit.

I soon set out again with hops, with a team of three horses, for New York city. This time I drove the horses through, carefully noting in a guidebook, where I could bait the team, and where put up for the night, all through the route, if I should conclude to team with oxen, should the war continue. Disposed of the hops and took on a load of cotton to bring to Boston, for four cents per pound. The new crop of hops was now in process of gathering, and I set about preparing two ox-teams for the purpose of teaming them. These teams consisted of six oxen and one horse each. For driver, hired Joseph Gowing of this town, now of Amherst, N.H. Price for carrying, four cents per pound. We set forward, and when at New Haven, there being no fear of the British, as was sometimes the case, put the hops on board a packet for New York. Freight on board the packet was one-fourth cent per pound and my fare both ways thrown in. Distance, 75 miles. I bought two loads of flour and left Gowing to load it and tend team. This flour was also sold to Bond, of this town, for $18 per barrel.

This business was continued while the war lasted, and sometimes I made the entire route with the ox teams. Jabez Gowing, now of Concord, Mass., was teamster on two of these trips. We always brought loads back — sometimes cotton, sometimes flour, and once glass.

I hope the following facts will not be thought too egotistical. At one time I had $5000 in gold to bring back for myself and others. The load consisted of flour. Before starting every barrel was inspected by a cooper who nailed the hoops anew, and pronounced it safe. I knocked in the head of one barrel, took out a quantity of flour, deposited the gold, put back the flour and passed over the barrel to the cooper, who said nothing but fastened in the head as usual. To be sure I kept an eye on that barrel until loaded; its place was in the centre of the load.

On the way home Jabez inquired, "What have you done with that money?"

"Oh, you had better not know."

"Why? I can't see what hurt it would do for me to know."

"Well, I can convince you that you had better not know. Nobody now knows where it is but myself. If I should tell you and it should be missing who should I suspect but you?"

"I don't want to know," said he.

I sold all but one barrel to William Bond.

"Why not every barrel?" said he.

"Oh, must carry one to my boarding place." The money came home safe.

In the month of November, at 8 o'clock in the morning, while my men were engaged in finishing a job of work, I was called upon to fit out two teams to go to New York, with great despatch. Benjamin Thompson came to me and asked if I could carry two loads of hops to market for him and start the next morning.

"Where are the hops?"

"Part at my press, part at Hopkins', and part at Jonathan Carter's."

"If you will deliver them all at my boarding place by 2 o'clock this afternoon, I will do it," said I.

"I will get them there."

Leaving men and teams to close up the work, I jumped on to my horse and made for Eben Jones' in Andover, and accosted him thus:

"I want you to drive your white-faced ox down to the blacksmith's at North Reading, and tell him to shoe him for me to go to New York, and charge the shoeing to me. Then drive him up to me and if I don't exchange with you, I'll give in the shoeing."

"I will go because the ox wants shoeing, but shall not trade with you."

I knew that ox was made for a traveller; but when he came up with him, Mr. Jones said, "Your oxen are now mated as well as they can be."

"I want you should tell me how you will trade," said I.

"I shall ask you $10," said he, "and your oxen will not look so well and will not fetch as much as now."

I placed the money in his hand. He in surprise said,

"What is the matter with your ox?"

"Nothing. He is as well as any ox in the world."

"Then what makes you mismate them?"

"Neither you nor any man can persuade me to start to New York with an ox whose toes turn out and whose knees bend in."

"That makes no difference," said he in true sympathy, "Now don't be so foolish as to throw away your $10."

"It makes a difference with oxen that work for me, and I am satisfied." He took the ox and went his way.

Thompson delivered the hops according to agreement,

and about 3 o'clock William Blanchard, Esq., came and asked me, "Can you start a load of hops for New York tomorrow morning for me?"

"Wait ten minutes and I will tell you what I can do." I stepped into the house and said to Mr. Harnden,

"Will you sell me those oxen I sold you the other day?"

"Yes, you may have them for the same I gave you."

"Will you let me your wagon to go to New York?"

"Yes," said he. I then told the 'Squire I would take his hops, if he would sell me his black and yellow oxen and advance $100 on the job, for I never liked to start on a journey without money enough to meet exigencies.

"What do you call the oxen worth?"

"$75," was the answer.

"You shall have them; but you could not have them one cent less."

It was dark when the hops were finished loading. I then rode down to Stephen Buxton's in Reading, knowing his cattle like a book. I found him in bed, but rapped at his window and said, "Mr. Buxton, I want you to get up, go to your barn and sell me your twin oxen."

"I will not get up to sell them to any man that ever was made; but you may take the lantern and go and take them for $75."

I went and yoked them, carried in the lantern and said, "I will take them if you'll throw in the yoke?"

"I will not throw in one cent. You may take it for your journey."

"I will," said I, "on these conditions, that you come after it when you want it." The yoke was never called for.

"You needn't unyoke them," said Buxton; "being twins they like to lay in the yoke as well as any other way." They were not unyoked till they came back from their journey.

I would not have it understood that I recommend leaving cattle over night in the yoke. There is not freedom enough enjoyed in that way.

These twins were great jumpers, and the man who
raised them kept them in yoke all summer on that account.
I reached home with them about one o'clock. Charged the
man who fed the teams to wake me in two hours. And
before the sun was in sight my three teams were all moving
on the road toward New York. The journey was prosperous,
and every ox came back as ready to work as when they
started. But the ox I put to Jones' had been several days
unable to work from lameness. "I never had so bad a trade,"
said he.

At another time, on our homeward journey, I was taken
sick, and with great difficulty reached the tavern at which I
intended to rest for the night. This general distress was
caused by exposure to humid atmosphere the day before,
getting chilled and then laying exposed to the cold. This
last misfortune should be carefully avoided after unusual
exposure.

This was Saturday night. On Monday, finding myself
unable to proceed, I hired a hand to drive, and was left
alone with my host and hostess. The former, after some
little conversation, proved to be an old schoolteacher who
had just married one of his pupils and was commencing
tavern-keeping at Farmington. They urged me, but urged
in vain, to have a physician called; they administered to the
best of their skill, by sweating and herb tea, and after four
days I was able to take the stage and overtook the teams at
Sturbridge after one day's ride, grateful for returning
health.

In April, 1814, I made a contract with Amos Binney, navy
agent, to draw a load of grape shot from Charlestown to
Commodore McDonald, in Vergennes, Vt. I brought the
load to Wilmington with four oxen and a horse. It weighed
6,700 lbs., at 3½ cents per lb.

Hearing that oxen were much wanted at Vergennes, I
bought two other yoke. So I started with four yoke of oxen
and a horse. They walked up the hills and through the mud

smart and easy. Thinking I might have some weak bridges to pass, I took with me a chain fifteen feet long to hitch on to the end of the wagon-tongue to save my team should the load break through. My route lay through Tewksbury, Lowell, North Chelmsford, Tyngsborough, Dunstable, Nashua, South Merrimac, Amherst, Mt. Vernon, corner of Lyndborough, New Boston, Francistown, Deering, Antrim, Hillsborough, Washington, Lempster, Unity, Claremont, Weathersfield, Cavendish, Mr. Holly, Ludlow, Trenton, Middlebury, &c., to Vergennes. I crossed the beautiful Connecticut River between Claremont and Weathersfield, where so straight was its course you might discern the bridge five miles distant, the river not varying its width.

On May 4th, I arrived at Vergennes, having undressed but twice on the journey. The shot were counted, found "all right," and I received my pay.

I sold my oxen, horse and harness, yokes and chains. The fifteen feet of chain sold for $5, double what it cost new. These things were wanted by the farmers, who had sold theirs to the government. The two yoke last purchased, brought $25 per yoke more than cost.

I started on the homeward tack the same night, with a market-man, and proceeded fourteen miles, and then, on foot and with occasional rides, I wormed my way home, a distance of one hundred and seventy-five miles. In Francistown, as the company were seating themselves at the breakfast table, there seemed a lack of room for me, my appearance being rather dirty and repulsive. The innkeeper seeing this, said, "Gen. Chandler, here, move about and let this man have a seat."

When loading into the stage, it was called out, before I could squeeze in, "No room for you, — no room for you." "Make room for him," said the innkeeper, "or I'll get in and make room for him; his money is as good as yours." Room was made, and I took my seat by old Gen. Chandler. He inquired, I thought, too minutely into my business and whereabouts, and said, "Wasn't you afraid to carry so much money?"

"No, not so much afraid of that as of not being allowed to sit down at the table." A general smile pervaded all faces, and from that time were chatting companions, he expressing regret that I was not going on to Boston.

There was a company drilling at Vergennes, among them was Joseph Southwick, of Danvers. He came to me as soon as allowed, and he was the only person there that I remembered seeing before. We were glad to meet. It is supposed he was soon after killed in an engagement that took place on the Lake, as he was not heard from afterwards. He was son of George Southwick, one of the eight martyrs that fell in our Revolutionary struggle at Lexington, on the 19th of April, and whose name is carved on the marble monument there. Joseph was born a few days after the death of his father.

I followed teaming hops, which then were extensively raised in this town, while the war continued, with commendable despatch. The whole arrangement was made with so much system, and the resting-places all designated with so much precision, that in three journeys there was not a variation of twelve hours. At one time, before setting out, I stated the hour we would be back. It was not ten minutes from the time set when we greeted the home band.

On starting out, old farmers said, our oxen would wear out before performing one journey, but they were so well cared for, night and day, that every pair came back every time better than they started, excepting one pair that went but once, because like Pharaoh's lean kine, the more they ate the poorer they looked.

NINTH LINK

War ended, and I still continuing to take hops to New York, but by an easier mode of transportation. The hops were put on board a sloop at Boston, and I took stage passage to dispose of them there. Several times I took hops to Philadelphia, and also to Baltimore.

One time on my stage journey from New York to Philadelphia, as the hostler was changing horses, I walked on ahead, and met a man that deserves notice, sure. He had driven an ox-team, loaded with tea, from Boston to Philadelphia. While reaching the latter place, peace was declared between the belligerent powers, and his load was not worth as much as when he started. Soon he received orders to take the load back. I inquired how far he travelled in a day. He said, "I don't know, but I can tell you so that you can give a pretty near guess. I have put up my oxen at that tavern yonder, for two nights and have not got there yet."

He was in a fair way to get there that day, and from what he told, I judged he advanced about two miles per day. This was called Jersey swamp, and some idea can be gained from it of Southern mud. The man seemed contented and his team looked well.

We now come to that important period in the history of an individual, on which hangs so much of future weal or woe. My marriage with CLARISSA EAMES, daughter of Nathan and Susanna Eames, was consummated Oct. 4, 1815. I was then 27 years old, and she 17. Commenced

housekeeping in what is termed the Ford house; now occupied by Edwin Blanchard.

Nothing noteworthy passed this winter. On March 20th,
David Hart, a hired hand, with myself, drove two loads of
trashy wood into Boston, and sold it for $10 per cord. It was
the highest I ever sold of any kind, being principally swamp
alders and blueberry bushes, not many sticks exceeding a
man's wrist in size.

Stoves, now so common, had just come into use, and the
prevailing opinion was, that nothing but small, dry wood
could be burnt in them.

This same Spring, a farm owned by George Flint, Esq., of
North Reading, was rented, and we moved on to it April
1st. Rent $100.

In the year 1816, that year so remarkable for its cold
spring, in which spots were seen on the sun, the corn crop
was nearly destroyed throughout New England by frost.
This produced a scarcity of pigs, as few farmers kept a hog
over winter. That year, pigs were killed that could not be allowed to live and were not fit to die. In demonstration of
this assertion, let me state a fact: one man actually brought
a large pig to David Hart and exchanged it for a small one,
about half the size of his, and gave 50 cents boot money, because the little one would eat less during the winter.

The first of August, there was a great cry for pigs. I said
to neighbor Batchelder, "We must go and get a drove of
pigs."

"Where shall we go?" said he.

I said, "Steer South-west and go till we get where corn
ripened, there we shall find pigs."

We started with $500 in our pockets. On the third day, at
night, friend Batchelder became discouraged, saying, we
could find no pigs, as every one we inquired of wished to
buy rather than sell. Said he, "We will call for fried pork for
supper tonight, and so find out whether hogs are kept in
this vicinity." But we were saved from that trouble by the

Innkeeper inviting us to go see his hog before going into the house. It was a grand one, a pattern for 600 weight.

We kept on till near York State line, where we made a stand. Mr. Batchelder, a plain, honest farmer, not a trading man, changed work with a farmer, preferring to work on his farm while he rode about buying up pigs.

At a store I bought fifteen of a farmer at 5 cents per lb., and called on the storekeeper to witness the bargain. Soon after I left, our farmer agent came up and bought the same pigs at 6¼ cts. per lb. Mr. Batchelder, hearing that two bargains had been made, feared hard thoughts. "Keep still," said I, "only take the carriage and bring the storekeeper down by the time the man gets here with his pigs, and there will be no trouble." He did, and the storekeeper took down the weights as told off, and made out a receipt, which I handed to the farmer to sign on receipt of his money at 5 cents per pound.

"The agent observed, "I bought those pigs at 6¼ cents."

"Well," said I, "these are the pigs I bought for 5 cents; if you have bought any of him for 6¼ cents, let him bring them on and I will pay for them." Here the matter ended without a dissenting word. This may show the impropriety of trusting strangers to trade for you, without looking sharply after them.

Another noteworthy circumstance. Old men told us that it made no difference whether a pig had his belly full or not, when weighed. Wishing to test the matter, I bargained with a widow, who lived in a retired nook, for a sow and two pigs, promising to come for them at noon the next day, I told her not to give them any dinner, and she was to give in all the swill they wanted for a meal. At the appointed time I went and weighed the pigs, and found their weight to be 70 lbs. each. I then gave them as much swill as they could eat, and again weighed them. This time they weighed 79 lbs. each. Next I weighed the sow, and then the swill-pail. After she had eaten her fill, she weighed 16 lbs. more, and the pail 16 lbs. less. This showed conclusively that feed weighs the same after eaten as before.

I sold that same sow in Sudbury on the banks of Concord river, to a tavern-keeper for 12½ cents per lb., showing that in an old hog the difference between an empty and a full belly, at this price, is $2. At Brighton, we were obliged to take special care to prepare the pens to hold pigs, this being the first drove ever driven there from New York State, although Smith & Reed, from Abington, came in soon after, with a drove.

In Brighton we retailed a hundred to our satisfaction. On our way toward Malden, Mr. Batchelder, a fun-loving man, observed a very homely, humpbacked pig, and wondered "what fool would buy it." When he had made what sport he would of the pig, I said, "If you will say nothing, I will sell that pig, when we get in Malden, higher than any other one, and tell only the truth — and not all of that."

We drove to the town pound, shut in the pigs and offered them for sale. To buyers we said, "take your choice for 12½ cts. per pound of all but one. I have one pig here I ask a shilling per pound for, of a particular breed."

"Which is he?"

The exclamation would be, "That will make a 600 hog. What breed is it?"

The answer was, "I don't know the name of the breed, but it is a very particular breed."

One man said, "I'll give 14 cts. per pound."

"I cannot take it."

He then said, "I'll give fifteen cents."

This was taken, and he drove off the pig. I never heard of him afterward; hope he made a fine hog.

Young men think of this when you hear particular breeds of cattle highly recommended. Be cautious about expending large sums, until experience proves their worth.

Once since then, I had a pig that much resembled the above named. I could not get rid of her so easily. Offering her to a man for $4 he cried out, "I won't have her in my hog-sty at any rate. If you would put her in my sty *for nothing*, I would not have her."

That pig was a profitable, if not more so, as any that I ever owned. She brought a littler of 9 pigs. I sold the whole for $55. The owners sold them when fattened at 12½ cts. per lb., amounting to $375.

For five or six years I was called upon, perhaps once a year on an average, by Master Parker and David to settle their animosities. After my departure the same evil spirit reigned in the old man, and Dave partaking of a share of it, and living in the same house, and working together, the spells would come when they could not speak to each other. After a while they would grow tired of it, and one would come up to me, tell the story of his wrongs, and entreat me to come down and bring about a treaty. In a very few days the other would come on the same errand, as I always expected, and then knowing both parties were ready and anxious for a settlement, I would go, carefully hiding from each, that the other had been to see me. Of course each considered himself the sold cause of my being there, and I presume they never learned to the contrary. When I arrived, I always had a talk with each one separately. There never was but one article in the treaty; it was always the same. Mr. Parker would say, "As David is my son it is his place to speak first, and he must come in to my room to do it." Dave was always ready to do it, when informed of his father's desire. I would then walk into the room with him and introduce them in this way, "Mr. Parker, your son has come to see you." "Good evening, father," Dave would say. The old man would jump up as spry as a boy, and shake hands most heartily with his son; and certainly they were, for the time being, as happy as their capacities would admit.

It always affords me pleasure to be the instrument of benefiting those who are so unfortunate as to possess such unhappy dispositions. If any person who reads this, finds himself possessed of a disposition leading to such unhappy results, I would entreat him to set about an amendment in his own soul. As much headway can be gained in laboring to improve the mind as in rooting briars out of the land.

On my last journey to New York, when about to leave, I went into a Broker's office to get $5000 exchanged. Noticed a man standing outside the counter, who appeared to have no business, but at the time, I supposed he had finished his business and was on some account waiting. He appeared to listen to all that was said, and heard the money told out.

"When do you leave for Boston?" said the broker.

"In the morning stage," said I.

"Who are your acquaintances in this city?" said he.

"Stebbins & Couch," was the answer.

"You could not be acquainted with better men," said he. "And if I leave word with them that I wish you to call here this afternoon, will you?"

"Yes," was the answer.

In the course of the afternoon Mr. Couch said to me, "The broker who changed your money for you has been here to inquire your character; and wants you to take $5000 to Oliver C. Wyman, State street, Boston. I told him he must pay your stage-fare to Boston, and he will do it." As I was about to leave, Mr. Couch added, "Do not be at that stage office after sunset, on any account."

When I had reached the door, he said again, "Don't you be at that stage office at sunset, let the excuse be what it will, now mind what I say."

From there I went to the broker's, took his $5000 and put it in my trunk with my $5000. He then gave me the money to pay the fare, which I took in my hand, and walked directly to the stage office, with trunk under my arm. It was situated in rear of a block of buildings with an arch leading to it. On entering I saw the very man who I had before seen at the broker's office. He was the man who it seems did business there, for he was behind the counter apparently engaged in writing. I stepped near and said, "Here is the money for my fare to Boston, and I would like to have the stage call for me at the sign of the Roebuck tomorrow. Please write 'A. G. Sheldon.'"

Wait one minute till I finish this letter, and I will wait upon you."

It was not quite sunset, so I seated myself near the door. I think I had not been seated a minute before a woman came in. She stepped up, paid her fare to Hartford, and had her name entered on the book to go in the same stage with me. I could see no reason why my name could not be written as well as hers; that increased my fears. I went directly up and laying down my pay beside hers, not stopping to have my name written, passed out after the woman. As I laid down the money he observed, "Only wait a half minute and I'll wait on you." I had told him my name.

"I'll wait no longer," said I, and started for my boardinghouse. Passing by the Mall, I heard footsteps coming fast behind and soon the same man clapped his hand on my shoulder, saying, "You made a great mistake when you paid your fare; if you will come back I will rectify it."

"I can't go back," said I.

"You had better go back, for you have made a great mistake, and I don't want your money for nothing."

This increased my fears. I brought my hand to my bosom suddenly, saying with vehemence, "take your hand from my shoulder or you are a dead man in one minute." He then loosened his hold and turned back.

The next morning I took the stage as expected, right glad to escape a robbery. Indeed, the whole reason the broker wished to send $5000 to Boston by me, was for fear of robbery, as several had been perpetrated about that time, on the mail. My journey was anything but pleasant. The stage run night and day. I was sleepy but dared to sleep but little, not knowing whether I was with friends or foes. My fear

was that he would describe me to some other rogue, and set
him out in the stage after me. I kept the trunk in my hand
when riding, and my foot on it while eating. Such not being
the case, I reached Boston safely and paid off the money.

In the course of the winter an event occurred that will
never be forgotten while memory retains her office. So narrow was the escape from a sudden death, or being wholly
smashed up, that when I look back upon it I am filled with
astonishment.

I set out with a team of 4 steers and a horse, and a load
of 15 feet of white pine wood, loaded 3 lengths on a sled,
one afternoon, to Reading market. Just after entering the
turnpike, south of Jerry Nichols' tavern, I stepped on to the
roller front of the sled; that instant the hind steers beginning to trot, I put one foot out on to the spire to start the
forward cattle, at the same time keeping hold of a stick in
the load with my left hand. The stick being short gave way,
pulled out and I fell my length on the spire, rolling off the
nigh side. My first thought was to brace my feet against the
wood to keep from going under the sled. So here I lay and
slid upon my back, so near the ox that ever time his foot
went back it touched my head. A large body of snow was
upon the ground, with deep footpaths for the cattle, and
hard, high ridges on either side. Imagine my feelings in this
perilous situation, with the team upon the run and but one
small chance of escape left me. I knew there was a footpath
just ahead where Munroe, a neighbor, crossed the turnpike
for water. So, bearing as much as possible toward the right
shoulder, when it struck the path I sprang for dear life, and
cleared the sled-road. I stopped the team and went back for
my whip, measured the distance and found it eleven rods.

"Bless the Lord, O my soul, and forget not all His
benefits."

TENTH LINK

My residence on the Flint farm embraced 13 years, during which I carried on butchering to considerable extent, trusting out meat largely, and in the course of that time I bought and paid for 515 acres young woodland.

Still owing some large debts, and hard times coming, on, creditors pressed their claims. I could not collect my debts fast enough to satisfy their demands, and a failure unavoidably ensued. My real estate was resigned into the hands of fourteen of my largest creditors, and the property appraised off at a very low rate, but sufficient to cancel all debts excepting $34. Had this $34 been paid, it would have cleared me from these debts, but I had no heart to ask any one to lend it to me. Afterward, when through the disinterested kindness of friends I had regained a footing and was able to do business again, I paid over $600 to those same creditors. When I placed those 515 acres of beautiful young woodland in the hands of these fourteen men, I expected they would manage so as to make themselves whole and save something for me. But such was not the case. They selected five of their number to manage the business. My feelings can be better imagined than described on finding that their whole aim was to have it sell as low as possible and buy it themselves.

An aged and venerable minister of the gospel being present at the auction, and seeing their management, said to me, "Sheldon, be perfectly honest yourself, but believe every man a devil."

A few incidents will show how the matter brought about, to me, unfortunate results. When a lot of nice young wood, of nine acres, was set up, it was struck off for $15. I persuaded the buyer to give me the refusal of it for a short time for $60. Before the time expired, I found a man that would advance me the money. In about three years, I had the wood cut off and sold it for $100, and then sold the bottom.

Another lot sold for $2.10 per acre, that has been worth since then $100 per acre.

One of the largest purchasers, not a creditor, told me that on the $500 worth, bought at that auction, he cleared $1000; and two of the creditors have since told me that on what they bought they cleared over $1000.

One lot lying by itself sold for $30. This sale was in 1830, and I have been credibly informed that the wood on this same lot, in the year 1860, sold for $900.

I would here insert an observation made by Edmund Parker, Esq., well known as a man of integrity and candor, who assisted the creditors in their business and who was their counselor. Said he, "If your creditors would let you alone three years, you could pay every debt and still have the foundation of as great wealth as any man in North Reading."

I should be untrue to myself did I not mention the names of three gentlemen to whose disinterested sympathy and assistance, I owe more than to all others. "A friend in need, is a friend indeed." Well have I seen this proverb verified in the troublous times that I have been called upon to pass through. These men were David M. Russell, then of Plymouth, N. H., now of Alabama; Ebenezer Emerson, of Reading; and Samuel W. Carter, of Reading. Nathaniel Parker, of Reading, would gladly have rendered assistance, but had not the means.

I fully believe in the common assertion that many, very many, men fail to make money by cheating their honest creditors; but I do know that an honest man would give but little for his choice, either to die or ask his creditors to take less than one hundred cents on the dollar.

Let me caution young men to look closely after their affairs, and always know how they stand, and be sure not to get so deeply in debt that if hard times come unexpectedly you may be able to handle your property and not trust it to the management of others.

My first introduction to the Baldwin family was by this circumstance. Going up to Milford, N. II., on business, I stopped for breakfast in Tyngsboro'. While eating, a stranger walked in and informed me that counterfeit $5 bills on Salem Bank were plentifully circulated in Andover. The news startled me, as I had $50 of that money with me and no other. I then offered the landlord one of the bills to pay for my breakfast. He refused, upon which I pawned my pocket book and departed.

I stopped next at Farewell Tavern, South Merrimack, and stated what had met my ears that day, when a tall, elderly gentleman asked my name, where I was from, and if I knew any one in Woburn. I replied, "I know Col. Franklin Baldwin."

"He is a brother of mine," he replied.

"Give this man some dinner, and I will pay for it," said he, to the Innkeeper, and turning to me continued, "I will exchange one of your bills, which no doubt are good, and give you money that is indisputable, and wish you to call and see me on your return."

The gentleman was no other than Cyrus Baldwin, of Chelmsford. Rest assured this was a great relief to me, being, as I was, among strangers, with no money but what had been condemned as counterfeit. Ever since this time, the name of Baldwin has sounded pleasantly in my ear.

My next interview with the family was by an appointment to meet James F. Baldwin, brother of Cyrus, in a woodlot of his. I bought the standing wood and timber, and one day going into the lot, met Mr. Baldwin, who said to me, "What are you going after now, Sheldon?"

"After the largest stick of timber in the lot," I answered.

"Do you expect to load it alone?"

"Yes, I do with the help of these oxen."

"How long do you expect it will take to load it?"

"If I have good luck, I expect to load it in an hour."

"If I thought you could load it in an hour, I would go back and see you do it."

"I think there is no doubt but what I shall."

He went back and sat down on a stump, took out his watch and said that it was twenty minutes from the time the oxen stopped when I started them again with the load all properly bound, ready for market.

He then said he was Engineer on the Boston & Lowell Railroad, and wished me to come to Boston and take a job.

"I have not means to carry on a job," said I.

"James Jaques said he would like to take a job with you," said he, "and if you will come and take one, and manage as well as you did loading this timber, if you do not make day wages, I will consider you, for I have power to consider contractors, if the work turns out more difficult than was expected."

The job of grading more than one and one-half miles of railroad, together with the stonework, was agreed upon, in company with Jaques. While with him the work dragged heavily; but subsequently he was exchanged for Isaac Flint of North Reading, and then the work went on satisfactorily. The job was taken of Jackson, Railroad Agent.

The next year Mr. Jackson said to me, "Sheldon I shall not let you any job on the railroad this year, because I want you to work by the day wherever and whenever you are wanted."

That season I worked forty oxen and fifty men for him by the day, nearly all the time; on an average more.

The third year I was employed by the same men in stonework and laying rails. On a certain occasion Jackson came along inspecting the work. One stone standing out prominently, he took occasion to find fault in sharp tones. I told him to wait fifteen minutes and I would show him the utility of its location. He waited, and then expressed himself with much satisfaction saying, "Sheldon, I will give you my word that you shall never pay anything for riding on this road, as long as your stonework holds good."

This declaration was as good as a bond to me, till the year 1861, long after Jackson's death.

I have hopes by an interview with the officers and agents on the road, to procure a lifelong ticket, for I have no doubt if they knew the conditions on which the promise was made they would freely award me the privilege of riding free.

In the spring of 1835, I received a letter from Jackson, desiring me to come to Boston, stating that he had a week's work for me to do. When there, he informed me that he wished me to ascertain what it would cost to move Pemberton Hill into salt water, north side of Causeway street.

After probing the hill in several places and walking over the ground as fast as an ox team would walk, to ascertain how many times they could go in a day, the result of my investigations was that it could be done for 25 cents per yard.

He then told me he was agent for a company and expected to buy the Hill, but the bargain was not concluded upon, but it would be in a few days; and further, said he, "I shall want you to do it by the day, for I don't expect to get any body to do it by the job quick enough, for it must be done in six months. If you should do the work, would you do it with oxen or with horses?"

"I shall do it with oxen."

"Give me your reasons why you should do it with oxen?"

"The job is short, and when done the oxen can be driven to Brighton and sold at a fair price, while horses would eat out half their bodies before we could make sale of them. And another reason, it does not cost so much to harness twelve oxen as it does one horse.

"Your reasons are good," said he.

I was in Boston four days. He paid me for a week's work and I came home.

Another letter was soon received requesting my presence in Boston. I repaired thither when he informed me that another man had offered to take the whole concern by the job, and said, "It is against our rules to have any work done by the day that we can let out by the job. Can't you take it by the job?"

"No," said I.

"Why not?" said he.

I answered, "Because I have already shown you that it will take $7000 to start the job, and $3000 more, making $10,000 before you will be willing to pay one cent, as you make payments monthly. And I have not got the money.

"Perhaps you will find someone who has the money to join you?"

I told him I should not try, and we parted.

Coming home I met Charles Carter, Esq., in Woburn. He said, "Are you going to do that job in Boston?"

"No," said I.

"Why not?"

"Because it is going to be let by the yard, and I have not the means to do it."

"How much money will it take?" said he.

"$7000 to start it, and $3000 more before we get the first payment."

"I can raise the money," said he, "if we can get a good job."

We looked at the work jointly and agreed to take it at 28 cents per yard. He furnished $1200, and I expended it all in oxen.

I started for Boston with the teams and met Carter a few rods beyond his house. He said, "I want the whole job to myself, and I will hire you to take care of the teams."

At that time I owed him four notes of $100 each, which he agreed to give me, if I would let him have the whole job, and work for him for $2.50 per day and he board me. I then said to him, "I will go back with you and take the notes."

"I can't give them to you tonight, for they are in the Bank, but you shall have them within forty-eight hours."

I then commenced work on the hill, it being May 5th, 1835. On the third day, Jackson came and said that the contract must be signed at 12 o'clock that day or the work stop.

Carter made for the office and I kept him company. Jackson read the contract and said, "Is that right, Carter?" He replied, "I think it is."

"Then there is nothing to do but to sign it."

"I don't think it worth while," said Carter.

"What does this mean, Sheldon," said Jackson, "didn't you tell me that that earth could be moved for 25 cents, and didn't I agree to give you 28 cents, and now you say you can't do it."

"I have said no such thing," said I.

"Then what do you say?"

"It can be moved full as easy as I ever expected," said I.

"I told you the teams could draw 12 loads per day, I now find they can draw 14 loads per day."

Carter then wished to see me alone. He asked me if I was willing to give up the last bargain and we do the work in company. I told him, "No."

Jackson soon came and told me to tell Carter, that if he would let me work the teams and men that afternoon, he would pay for the work.

Mr. Jackson and Baldwin were both on the work the whole afternoon, and at night Jackson said to me, "I am satisfied you can do all you have told me and more too. You may buy of Carter every ox that you want, and every thing he has that you want, and tell him he shall have his money next Tuesday. If you had the money, would you do the job?"

"Yes," said I.

"You shall have it. Notify the men that you shall want them all Monday morning."

By an early start I was at Jackson's house before sunrise on Monday morning. "Do you want me to step into Carter's shoes," said he, "and find money and you do the work and have half the profits?"

"Yes; but one thing more, if there is a loss in it I will lose only my time."

To this he finally agreed, saying, "You always make me do just as you please. Now, as soon as you get men and teams to work, come to my office."

When at the office, "Now," said he, "I have a short lesson to give you: remember, this work is to be done on your judgment, not on mine. If I think you are doing wrong and tell you so, don't you alter unless I convince you of the wrong. Don't say, you should not have done this or that if I had not told you so. Some people think because they find funds to do a job they must dictate, when they know nothing about it, and thus spoil the work. Remember, this job must be done in six months. How much money do you want today to buy oxen with at Brighton."

He then gave me a check for $1000. I started a man to North Andover, to Ingalls' the yoke maker, to bring yokes and bows enough for thirty yoke of oxen. I then proceeded to Brighton and bought ten yoke of cattle that day. Ingalls was at my place in Boston before sunrise the next morning, with more yokes than I sent for, but no more than was wanted.

We now had about half as many oxen as needed, but as many as we had carts for then. As carts could not be made as fast as wanted, I procured two men of sound judgment, — Abner Marion, of Burlington, and Eben Emerson, of Reading, — and sent them about in the neighboring towns to buy good secondhand carts and wagons. They succeeded well, making no bad bargains, both being careful men.

I then issued the following advertisement:

WANTED — TWENTY YOKE OF THE BEST WORKING OXEN, AT PEMBERTON HILL, BOSTON, FOR WHICH A

FAIR PRICE WILL BE PAID IN CASH. NONE BUT THOSE
THAT CAN TRAVEL ON PAVEMENTS NEED BE OFFERED.

This was the season of the year when farmers in the
vicinity of Boston were finishing up their heavy spring
work; consequently I had as many oxen offered as wanted,
having no occasion to go out to buy.

I boarded my first week at Glasier's Tavern; paid my bill
every morning and inquired if I could board there another
day. I wore my teamster's blue and white striped frock, and
in this disguise could hear at table many curious observations on the moving of Pemberton Hill with oxen.

One stated, "These oxen will have their tongues out as
long as your arm, and in three weeks he won't be able to
get them through the streets."

Another said, "I understand the man came from Wilmington, a sandy town, and I expect he don't know but that
oxen can travel on pavements as well as in Wilmington sand."

As the work was a novel job, many spectators were attracted to the scene of operations. They were of all grades,
from the highest to the lowest, among them many country
teamsters, whip in hand. To hear the observations, I one
day ascended with the throng on the back side of the hill, in
my usual disguise, and took my stand by the smartest looking man in the foremost rank, which was then several
courses deep, when he thus addressed me, "This is a
tremendous piece of work."

"It looks to me to be so," I answered.

"I understand that the man who has taken this job, has
agreed to do it in six months; do you know if it is so?"

"I understand he has," was my answer.

"Then he is a fool, let him be who he will. He can't do it in
three years, if he employs all the men and teams he can
work on it."

In this connection it may not be uninteresting to give a
description of Pemberton Hill. The whole area, including
Streets adjoining, was upwards of four acres, and it made

in the water, eight acres, fourteen feet deep. Depth of hill, from the highest point, was sixty-five feet and ten inches. This was the point where Gardner Green's green house stood. Six dwelling houses and other outbuildings, besides immense shrubbery, together with several English elms that were carried to the navy-yard, were sold from the ground. One gingo tree, an exotic, and I expect the only tree of the kind in this country, I was offered $300 to move and warrant to live one year. I thought at that time, that it contained about two feet of cord wood, and it being in the month of June, I dared not undertake it. However it was moved, and now stands on the Common, near the State House and is thriving.

These buildings had been the residences of distinguished gentlemen — Gardner Green, Dr. Lloyd and Gov. Phillips. There were two other beautiful brick buildings on Somerset street sold and torn down, whose owners I never knew. I will now note a few things by me deemed curiosities.

The Dr. Lloyd house stood on the lowest ground of any, with a well thirty feet deep and not a drop of water in it. The Gardner Green well stood a few rods from it on a little higher ground. The top of the water in this well was thirty-five feet higher than the base of the ground at the cut near the well. When working very near the water gushed out and formed a brook that ran down to Hanover street. As we watered our cattle from it, the stream would stop running in the day but fill up and run again in the night. Opposite the head of Court street, about five feet from the surface we struck a flat stone. On turning it a well thirty feet deep was discovered. On listening, running water could be distinctly heard. We ascertained that it came in, fifteen feet from the top and run directly out at the bottom. Our grading was five feet below the flat stone. We filled up with clay, the water still running, puddled it in so compactly that in one night the well was filled to overflowing. The next day it was filled to the top, that kept the water down.

This place is now called Pemberton Square.

Near the centre of the green enclosed by the Square, after taking off about fifty-five feet of solid gravel, a heavy load of gravel passing, suddenly all four of the wheels dropped to the hub. The gravel was quickly shovelled out of the wagon, when on procuring an iron rod, the mud was found to be common marsh mud, fifteen feet deep, of an oval form and entirely covered with gravel. This must have been done by some convulsion in nature. At Jackson's suggestion we excavated the mud, six feet in depth and filled with gravel.

When at the Phillips' place we found an iron door in the cellar, that led to an arch about twelve feet wide on the base, fifty feet long and nine feet high. I remember well measuring it, and found plenty of room for sixteen large oxen and space to feed them; but fearing they would not do so well in this subterranean cell as in a barn, did not put it to that purpose. This arch was made of brick, sixteen inches in thickness, so firmly cemented that much labor was required to prepare it for loading into our carts. So true it is, one man builds and another demolishes. Of the original design of this subterranean arch, I leave my readers to judge for themselves, as I do for myself. It occurs to my mind that rich men do not always comply with the letter of the law, especially when they have a convenient place in which to secrete smuggled goods.

From the cellar of one of the brick houses an iron door opened into a sepulchre or tomb, from which, I think, fifteen coffins, large and small, were taken the night before we had leave to occupy it. This information was received from Mr. Hersey a man in city employ, who helped convey them to another tomb. On the outside, on the tomb were beautiful cultivated flowers. However others may think on the subject, it is quite ungenial to the feelings of the writer to have dear, departed friends lying under a dwelling-house or so immediately connected with it. The most proper place to lay the dead for their last resting-place is in the common burying-ground.

Some time previous, a crew of Spanish pirates were cap-
tured and brought into port in Boston. They were subsequently tried, and Bernardo De Soto and four others were
condemned and sentenced to suffer the penalty of the law
due to their crimes, *viz*: to hang by their necks till they
were dead.

While in jail, awaiting their doom, one of the number, to
speed on his release from earth, pierced his arm with a
piece of glass, causing much blood to flow and such a state
of debilitation that the poor deluded man was carried to the
place of execution in a chair, and there sat to hear the service and have the halter placed round his neck, and dropped with the rest. Oh, sad, sad and mournful affair. Yet we
would not wish to have capital punishment abolished, but
rather carry out the Scripture rule, "He that sheddeth
man's blood, by man shall his blood be shed." No, the world
is not good enough to do away with capital punishment yet.

The pirates were hanged on a gallows erected on my land
by the United States Marshal. I had built three barns tem-
porarily for the use of my oxen. There were fifty tied in one
barn, twenty-five in a row. The teamsters were set to guard
them, and two men were stationed on the top to keep spectators off, each with a pitchfork, and with directions, if they
failed, to have the cattle turned out. Rowdies and ill-bred
boys pressed so hard upon the men on top, and beginning
to throw stones, that they shouted to the teamsters below
to turn out the oxen. No sooner said than done, when one of
the top men jumped off, crying, "Now you may all go to h—l
if you please." The roof was covered as fast as possible,
when, crash, down came the whole frame, breaking one
man's arm. No teaming work could be done in Boston on
such days as this, or on holidays.

That night application was made to me for a team to
carry the pirates' lifeless bodies to the Catholic Burying-
ground, Charlestown, and with them an Irishman killed on
the railroad. I accordingly sent one man with a yoke of

oxen, and six men for guard. The oxen, passive before, expressed fear as soon as the bodies were put in, and could be restrained from running only by two men going before them with clubs. Whether they were frightened by something natural or supernatural, is beyond my conjecture. Perhaps, like Balaam's ass, they saw that which human eyes could not discover.

The next day I made out a bill like this,—"United States Marshal, Dr., To A. G. Sheldon: To damage done to barn, . . . $50;" and presented it to the Marshal. He looked at it and said, "I can pay no such bills." I then requested the use of a slip of paper, pen and ink, and then wrote,—"United States Marshal, Dr., To A. G. Sheldon, To use of land to hang 5 pirates, and damages sustained thereby, . . . $75." This suited him, and he paid the money.

ELEVENTH LINK

We will now return to the work on the hill. In about ten days Dr. Lloyd's house was sold at auction. I bid it off, moved my chattels in that night, and next morning sixty Yankee men took breakfast in it. For shovelling, we employed Irishmen wholly, they boarding themselves.

When Dr. Shurtleff, our nearest neighbor, saw that the house was sold for what he called a shanty, he expressed many fears lest he should be troubled with noise. He said, "I could not have thought that of Patrick T. Jackson, that he would allow the house to be sold for that purpose."

Subsequently he inquired, "When are you going to get your men on, Sheldon?" I said, "Have you been disturbed by their noise, Doctor?"

"No, I have not heard any noise."

"The morning after I bought the house, sixty men ate breakfast there and have boarded there ever since."

"If that be the case," said he, "I'll borrow no more trouble about the noise."

The doctor proved himself a kind friend and neighbor, coming in often with Jackson and Baldwin to dine on baked beans. He was extremely fond of brown bread and butter, which we had of an excellent quality; and when any of the men were hurt or required medical aid, he tendered his services without remuneration.

About the first of June our ranks were filled. The whole number of oxen being one hundred and twenty-six; whole number of hands about two hundred and fifty when at the highest pitch,— sixty Yankees and one hundred and ninety Irish.

We soon found from experience that long and narrow wagons run the best. What may be called sloven bodies were used with a sideboard so fixed that it could be quickly started with two iron bars, and the entire load slide off in about a minute, on an average. One man would drive two yoke of oxen with a wagon and two yards of gravel, while it took two men and two yoke of oxen to carry the same amount in carts. To satisfy the curious, we had one of the wagon loads weighed on the hay scales, weight over seven tons.

In my employ were forty teamsters. I began to realize how much the work depended on their holding on, when I found the country farmers would try to hire them for haying, with the promise of $1.50 per day.

One man, who had charge of the barn and cattle feed, was used as a reporter, and I do not think that the men ever mistrusted he held that office. One night he said, "The teamsters have all agreed to leave as soon as they get their pay for the month of June."

I then began to try my brains to discover what could be done. When payday came I called them all in together and said, "You know I hired you for the whole job. But it is dirty, unpleasant work compared with haying; and I know wages are some higher than when I hired you. Now boys I shall give every one of you $26 for the month of July, which is $6 more than I agreed to pay, but for my own security shall keep back $5 of this month's wages until the job is completed."

The next day the reporter told that they had all agreed to stay, to a man. They said, "The old man was so good without knowing they had agreed to go away, it would be too bad to leave him."

I will here acknowledge this was the most trying circumstance in the whole job, and when it was settled my uneasiness subsided.

Now another difficulty arose. The dust proved insufferable to those who lived on the streets through which we passed, and much annoyed the cattle and men. After some consultation with individuals, and with the Mayor, it was decided that I should pay $1.50 per day toward sprinkling the streets and they would keep them wet, much for the comfort of the men and the cattle's feet.

About this time Mr. Jackson said to me, "Sheldon, if you could have something extra, could you do this work in five months instead of six."

"Yes, I think I could."

"Remember," said he, "you are trading for me and yourself, while I am trading for the company. How much extra shall I give you to do it in five months?"

"Let me think till morning and I will tell you."

In the morning he said, "Have you made up your mind?"

"Yes, give me an extra $1000 and it shall be done in five months."

"At noon I will give my answer," said he.

At noon he told me he would comply with my terms and give $1000.

"Now Sheldon," said he, "you may work as hard as you please, but don't kill yourself. This job has been the least trouble to me of any job of such magnitude I ever had anything to do with."

The commencement of this monster job was in May. The first shovel full of dirt was thrown out on the morning of May 5, between 7 and 8 o'clock; and the last shovel full on Oct. 5, between 7 and 8 o'clock in the morning. As the owners of this land feared hard times were coming they hurried it into market. Advertisements were seasonably put out and the sale commenced at auction, Oct. 6. The ground was previously laid out in suitable house-lots, walks and streets; each enclosed with narrow strips of board, with a strip of common land in the centre. The conditions of the sale were, that every house should be built according to the plan then laid out. Strange as it may seem to those unacquainted with city operations, the highest house-lots sold for $7 per foot.

But I find my pen has run ahead, beyond the straight line of my story. I will now go back to say that as soon as sufficient new land could be made, a temporary blacksmith's shop was erected, where we could do our ox-shoeing, mending chains, &c. Two blacksmiths were hired, Stephen Smith and John S. Perry. They proved excellent workmen, and I thought sometimes vied with each other in the shoeing business. By employing two smiths, and keeping shoes on hand an ox would be kept in the cage but a very few minutes, and of course save time. Neighboring farmers from Brighton, Brookline, Charlestown and Chelsea, finding my oxen traveled so well on pavements, would call at our shop when they came in with their teams to get them shod. We were able to do considerable of this kind of work.

As I have heretofore spoken of the number of men employed, I cannot be so ungallant as not notice the fair sex. For housekeepers I employed constantly one young man, Henry O. Holly, and Caroline Foster of Wilmington, and Catherine Jones of New Hampshire, for cooks, besides one other girl as help; several different girls being employed at different times. Before purchasing the Dr. Lloyd house, the men took their meals at Victualing Cellars; some at Sawyer's Cellar on Charlestown Square, and some at Campbell's on North Market street, and slept in the barns on the hay.

The personal property on the Hill at the commencement of the work was sold at different times, and sometimes they were so remiss in moving it as greatly to annoy us.

Once when Jackson was about to make another sale he said, "Sheldon, you know we have been plagued with the owners not removing their property out of our way as soon as agreed upon. Now I have understood they have a right to let it remain, and all I can get is the damage, and it will

cost more than it is worth to get that. Can you contrive any
way to oblige them to take it away on the day specified."

I said, "Yes, sell them as much of the property as shall be
removed in a given time, and be sure to have this specified
in the articles of sale."

"That will do it. And now whatever is left when the time
expires, I will give to you for this idea." This was carried
out to the letter. Mr. Jackson desiring to carry out this rule,
wished me to appropriate all property remaining beyond
the limited time. I allowed them to carry off till midnight of
the last day, then forbade their taking another stick. The
teamsters, I think as many as six, were angry and determined on filling their carts again, but seeing my men, who
had been notified, issue from the house like a cloud, they
quit and drove off. I would recommend this course to those
who sell standing wood, as better for buyer and seller too,
for the young sprouts are greatly injured by being trodden
down or gnawed by the teams, and the buyer is stimulated
to an honorable exertion to do business in its proper time.

In the early part of the work, David Golden, an Irishman, offered terms for a job of shovelling. Having an inveterate dislike to subcontracts, I declined, but at a strong
invitation from Jackson, agreed to it. However, it proved a
real bother, Mr. Jackson thinking the same, and I made
another bargain with him to quit in three weeks. The time
expired at noon. The money was procured, it was $823, and
paid him at 11 o'clock; he appointing a certain place to pay
off his men. At 20 minutes before 12, I informed them their
time was up, and they might go for their pay. They went,
but nothing could be found of him, nor has he been heard of
from that day to this by me.

This season a great change in prices current was experienced. The Eastern Land Speculation had turned to a
"consuming fire," that seared and scorched speculating
men. The scant crops of hay and grain raised their prices.
For the first load of hay, I paid 68 cents per hundred; the

last, $1.25. For the first meal, 83 cents per bushel; the last $1.40. For the first shovelers, 83 cents per day; the last $1.17. Flour rose in proportion.

As the job wore away, less teams could be employed, and many of them were sold on the ground. One pair was sold long before they could be spared, to Peter C. Brooks, millionaire, and so well pleased was he with them, that ever afterwards he would buy of no other man; and in fact every pair that were driven by a middling teamster sold for as much as was paid for them.

Near the close of the work, Mr. Jackson came along one day and said, "I never like to see people dress above their business, but you do not dress as well as your workmen."

"I know that," said I, "but there is one consolation, I know who is able to give me a suit of clothes."

"How much will a suit of clothes cost you?"

"About $50," I answered.

He then filled out a check for $50, and gave it to me.

"Now get a suit of clothes to suit yourself," said he.

The clothes being finished, I put them on Monday morning and went into his office and accosted him with, "Good morning, Mr. Jackson."

"Good morning," said he; "I thought some gentleman had come into my office. Your clothes suit very well, I am glad to see you look so well in them."

"And I too am well pleased with them," said I, "but I think I had better lay them aside till I have finished this job."

"They are your own, wear them when and where you please."

The work being all done, hands paid off, oxen and chattels all sold, bills paid and receipted, nothing now remained but to get the estimate of the measurement from the Engineer and then take our pay. This was put off a week at a time for three successive weeks, when Mr. Jackson went with me to his office and demanded the estimate.

"You shall have it one week," said the Engineer.

"Can't you tell us something near what it will come to," said Jackson; "Mr. Sheldon wants to know whether he is going to have any more money or not."

"I have gone so far," said he, "I know there will not be less than two hundred thousand yards."

As we rode back, Mr. Jackson observed, "now Sheldon you will never need any more of my help. Two hundred thousand yards will give $20,000 profit. You will have $19,000 left, and that is enough for you to begin with."

The Engineer's name was Fuller. The first Engineer on the work was named Putnam; he left and went into the United States Service, and Fuller took his place.

A week later I was in Jackson's office when the sealed estimate was brought in. On looking it over Mr. Jackson exclaimed, "A fool riding on a trotting horse would guess nearer than this."

"What is it?" I inquired.

"Only one hundred thousand and eighteen yards."

Believe me this was in truth a thunderbolt; my thoughts were too big for utterance. Jackson, turning to me, said, "Sheldon, don't feel so back; you shall have $1000 if I don't have a cent. You have worked like an Indian."

"That is better than nothing," said I, "but a man would feel better to have $19,000 of his own earnings, than to have $1000 given to him."

George M. Dexter was then employed to take the measurement where it had been filled into the water. This resulted in an estimate that gave $2700 profit, of which Mr. Jackson took $1000, leaving me $1700.

Let me here tell a story or two and then conclude the link. I was one day at Brighton for the purpose of selling some cattle. I sold three and received the money. I put $118 in a purse, my usual receptacle, in the right pants pocket, and about $5 in change in the left. In those days the barroom at the Market Hotel was crowded as densely as it could be, just before the dinner bell rung. Then there would be a continuous rush. That day I happened to feel something at my left pocket, and dropping my hand as quickly as possible, caught hold of a man's wrist. I then heard the change rattle and felt something touch me below which no doubt was another man's hand into which the purse was dropped, and at the same time I called out, "A man's got my purse; he ain't got it now; he's dropped it into another man's hand;" and at once clutched the robber by his neckerchief. The zealous Wardsworth, barkeeper, with remarkable agility, leaped over the bar and over the shoulders of the men, so thick were they huddled together, and was the first after me to seize him. Luckily for me that the robber did not take the purse that was in the right-hand pocket. That night he found a lodgment in Cambridge jail. For three successive weeks, Peter W. Ray, keeper of a hotel in Boston, came to Brighton on market days to confer with me respecting this case. He urged me to say what I would take and not appear before the Grand Jury. My reply was, "The case is in the hands of the Commonwealth; I am nothing but a witness, and shall not attempt to settle this business at any rate." After a few days a bondsman was obtained for the sum of four hundred dollars, I think, and the well-dressed robber, with rings on his fingers, was released from confinement. When the Court sat, no robber appeared, and the bond was forfeited.

The Saturday following this robbery, I was at Cambridge Cattle Market, and noticed two men ride up in a chaise and wait in the barroom, apparently without any particular business. This excited my suspicions. My horse being harnessed and about ready to start, John Randall, drover, from Vermont, asked which way I was going. Finally I decided to come through West Cambridge, and bring him along with me, and look at his working cattle, as at that time I dealt in oxen. On the road, I perceived those same gentlemen, in their chaise, following behind. I stopped at West Cambridge

Hotel, and went down into the lot to examine the cattle. When I came back at dark I found the same men sitting in the barroom, and this increased my fears much. How to evade them was the next question. I summoned up my wits, found my way into the kitchen and told the maid to ask the landlord to come in there, and added, "But don't say, 'a man wants to see you,' only say 'please come in here.'" He came accordingly and I asked him, "Have these two gentlemen who are waiting any business here?"

"Not that I know of," was his answer.

I stepped back to the barroom, bid Randall good night and started off, but soon found that they were following behind again. Coming to a fork in the road, and feeling certain something must be done immediately to get clear of them, as night was setting in, I stopped my horse by the way side and jumped out to busy myself in unbuckling and buckling some of my harness. They rode past and took the right-hand road, went a few rods and stopped. I waited a few minutes, but as they did not start I thought it best to turn back, and said to the landlord, "It is so dark and rainy I shall not go home tonight." I never heard any more of them, and never doubted their intent to take my life. I was careful after that occurrence not to be on the road from Brighton at night, until after Court set.

In the month of March, I went one evening across what is called, "Hundred Acre Meadow," which was then covered with ice. In returning, the weather being foggy, I could not exactly see my course and steered too far North, which carried me on to the river. Down went the horse and one side of the sleigh, while I scratched out on to the ice and there lay, not daring to get up or stir an inch. The water flowed under me; what was to be done. I hallooed loud and long, till fortunately the noise waked Jonathan Gowing from sound sleep, and he came to his door and answered "Hallo." Finding my call responded to, I called out, "Rope, rope,— River, river." Mr. Gowing proceeded to uncord his bed, and then with a lantern, in company with his two sons, made the best of their way to the spot which was distant about half a mile. I grasped the rope they threw me, and was drawn from my watery bed to a place of safety. One of the boys then fastened the rope to the collar of the horse, his head still sticking out of the water, and we drew both horse and sleigh to hard ice. Had this occurred on the downward trip, with the sleigh loaded with men, the consequences might have been more disastrous. I had been employed with them the previous week in looking out a location for Salem and Lowell Railroad.

TWELFTH LINK

The following winter I employed several yoke of cattle with some of the best men, in lumbering.

At the opening of spring, I repaired again to Boston to dig cellars on Pemberton Hill, by teaming the gravel to the same place, filled the year before. This occupied about two months, for which $3834.25 was paid me, being quite satisfactory. Mr. Dexter took the engineering of this work, and I likewise kept the cart measure, and when the whole was summed up, there was only $9 difference. Dexter observed, that two men measuring it in a half-bushel could not come out nearer. Dexter's measurement was the largest.

Our teams were now ferried over to East Boston, to street building. Here we made five miles of streets and then returned to Boston. Here we made Lowell, Nashua, Haverhill, Andover and Billerica streets, working by the day for Jackson. My pay was $5 per day. The men were paid by him as cheap as I could hire them.

I will now take a peep at the Lowell Railroad again. The first track was laid with a trench wall of two feet in depth under the rails. Mr. Jackson one day said to me, "Sheldon is there anything better than small stones for a trench under the rails?"

"Yes, there is," said I.

"I should like to know what?"

"Coarse gravel that the frost has nothing to do with."

"I should like to see some such, if there is any," said he.

"There is plenty of it near the canal locks in Wilmington.

It is of the kind that will not dirty your hands. Take up a handful and it appears like smashed stone from the size of a cranberry down to half a shot and finer. You may handle it and throw it away and it will not leave dirt on your hands."

"Get into our carriage," said Jackson, "and we will go and examine it." When on the ground, he and Baldwin did examine for themselves, when Baldwin said, "Mr. Jackson, this is indeed pulverized stone. Sheldon is right; there is no dirt in it."

They soon commenced using that kind of earth, when Baldwin came again and said, "Sheldon, we have decided on your kind of gravel, but it costs too much to make it hard. Now will you go with me and see if you can contrive to do it cheaper?"

We went up to West Medford, where we found sixteen Irishmen pounding down the gravel with mauls.

He says, "Now this costs us $6 per rod to pound it down. Now can you tell of a cheaper way?"

I answered, "Put in four heavy oxen and their sixteen feet will do more than sixteen mauls."

He then hired Noah Johnson's four oxen to use one hour, and acknowledged his belief that those four oxen had done more than sixteen Irishmen could.

Jackson desired me to take charge of the job, and to use the best of my skill in any process of hardening it I might choose. Work being about finished up in Boston, I speedily procured a pair of millstones, put in an axletree and spire, and run them night and day, changing teams as often as necessary. To facilitate business, the gravel was brought on cars, and by the use of millstones the hardening process was reduced from $6 to 63 cents per rod.

I would now like to state a few things of which I claim to be the originator, and which I wish all to understand.

I will now take a leap back to the time when I cut off the Foster lot, in 1812. This was the first time I had hired men to cut wood by the cord. Every one of them was charged to be sure to pile every split stick bark side up. This I learned when quite young by loading wood that had lain nearly a year. I found that a stick laid bark side up would be bright and dry, but those laid otherwise would be dark colored and heavy; and if it had lain over a year water would frequently settle between the bark and the wood, causing the bark to slip off. One old, experienced wood-chopper receiving the same orders, went on to his work. Going into the lot a few days after, I was struck with wonder to see what pains he had taken to lay every stick bark down.

"Why did you pile the wood that way," said I.

"Why," said he, "I knew you was a very particular man, and I had forgotten which way you wanted it, but thought it could not be bark up."

"I will now tell you so that you will never forget again. Remember, when God created cattle he put the hide and hair on the outside to protect them from the weather. So when he made trees to grow he made bark grow on the outside to protect the wood. And wherever you see bark bruised off, there the wood will rot.

This occurrence was fifty years ago, and became the sport and sneer of wood-choppers; but now, nineteen out of twenty pile their wood bark-side up.

I likewise claim to be the originator of iron axletrees for ox-wagons in the New England States.

Deacon John Symmes was builder of the woodwork, and Marshall Symmes, his brother, made the ironwork. They both expressed many fears that under heavy loads, they would break in frosty weather. The custom had been to punch a hole through the axletree to fasten on the body. This served to weaken the axle, and cause a liability to break. To remedy this I had the body fastened with two bolts, passing each side the iron axle, instead of one going through it. This wagon was built in 1816. I now have the same axletrees with the hubs of the forward wheels, in good running order, a period of forty-six years.

The use of dry, loose, stone gravel for railroad trenches, as before stated, was through my observation. For carriage roads it surpasses anything known. Blue gravel treads down quick and makes a pretty road at first, but as soon as rain falls it becomes muddy. In short, it is nice for walks and streets any where; for I know of nothing that will grow in it but pitch pines. To cover grave lots with it a few inches deep, is a sure preventative to weeds and fern, keeping the ground neat and clean, without labor or attention from year to year.

I was first to practice laying railroad bearings two and a half feet apart in steady of three. This I consider a great improvement, and is universally adopted by all railroad companies, as far as I have any knowledge. My first experience of this was in 1834, when constructing a piece of railway through the farm then owned by Eldad Carter, Wilmington. It was considered a hard piece, and we were afraid rails could not be made to stand. I tried the experiment of placing the bearings six inches nearer than usual and found it succeeded admirably. After the cars had run awhile, Baldwin said to me, "Sheldon, 'tis said you have made the best piece of road from Lowell to Boston. The Engineer says, that if he were blindfolded in Boston or Lowell, he could tell when he struck that piece of way."

"Where is it," said I.

"'Tis that bad piece you were so afraid of."

"Do you know the secret of that road?" said I.

"No; only we thought it was so miry and bad you put in your best work."

"The whole secret is in the bearings being six inches nearer together than others are," said I, "and if you observe you can see the rails will spring when the cars run over where the bearings are three feet apart."

"If that be the case, I will go up and examine it," said he.

He did go, and examined for himself and became satisfied that the latter plan was a great improvement and a great saving of rails, as well as engines and cars.

Again: I have discovered that abutments of bridges should be set two feet below the surface, and the basement stones so placed that the front line of the abutment should rest on their centre. All front abutment stones should be laid without a pinner in front. They should have a good bearing and not need a pinner. In taking down abutments laid by others, to relay them, I have found that the main difficulty consisted in having pinners in front. The jar had crumbled them into small pieces. All bank walls or abutments having earth behind them, should be bartered at least one inch and a half per foot.

"Necessity is the Mother of Invention." I once had some stones to move that averaged about five tons each. I hardly knew how it could be done as wheels could not be used, the pass not being wide enough. As I stood thinking upon it for a moment, it occurred to me that good, straight, rye straw, spread crosswise of the path, would help the drag. On trying this plan I found that it worked to a charm. The hotter the sun shone, the easier the drag would slide, and I found one good yoke of oxen would slip along with five tons comfortably. Twenty-five pounds of straw to the rod will make a good, fair road.

To those who have board-timber to cut at a distance from mill, I would say, cut it in the month of August, or first of September, and peel the bark off. This will lighten the timber about one half, and the bark proves good fuel. I have carried two feet to market on top of a load of six feet of hard, green wood, and sold it as high as if it had been all hard wood. The difference in drawing these logs compared with new fallen logs is not small.

I claim the first invention of wagon springs. When I first peddled meat, springs on market-wagon seats were unknown, and under wagons too. The wagon body set on the axletrees, as wood wagons set in these days, and the box in the front end was the seat for the driver. My health declined, and, strange to say, I could not eat without difficulty. At length the trouble increased so much that I could not eat at all while in a sitting posture and was obliged to take my meals standing. Speaking one day with Dr. Nathan Richardson, that eminently skillful physician, he said it was produced wholly by the continuous jar of riding, as my route lay through country towns, sometimes to the extent of forty-five miles per day over very rocky roads. I then planned some springs, very much like those now called grasshopper springs, and Jonathan Batchelder of North Reading made them. These springs though rude and simple had a salutary effect, and health was soon regained. John Sweetser, an extensive butcher, was ahead of me in one respect, inasmuch as he used a cushion on his hard seat before I did. This was the first on I had ever seen used. It was very much sneered at by Salem butchers, for in that day comfort did not enter into the reckoning.

In December 1834, in company with Isaac Flint made a contract with Jackson for cedar ties enough for seven miles of railroad. After reconnoitering the neighboring towns we came to Middleton, where plenty of cedar could be taken from a swamp when sufficiently frozen, and to facilitate the road to mill, it was necessary to cross Middleton Pond. This was December 19th, and one more cold night was deemed sufficient to make the Pond bearable. Our teams were at South Woburn, now Winchester, making preparations for an early start, and so well did we succeed that the next morning at sunrise a load of cedar might be seen crossing Middleton Pond on its way to mill. Before the opening of Spring a choice lot of cedar was collected there, more than enough to fill our contract; the surplus was readily taken at the same price.

This winter was noted for its storms all falling in the night or on Sundays. Only one half day was so foul as to prevent work. I could hardly believe that there had been a winter, so universally fair had it been, only as I knew such was the fact. The work was begun December 20th, the first day the ice would admit, and finished March 20th, on which night a warm rain come on that would have, at any rate, precluded our doing anything further.

Much of the lumber being too good for ties, was worked into boards, and a good winter's work realized. Twenty oxen and twenty men were employed; and not only in Middleton, but in Wilmington, North Reading, Reading and South Reading, swamps were scoured for cedar, and besides our ties nearly one hundred thousand feet of boards were supplied.

In 1836, in company with Joseph Richardson, of Andover, agreed to contract for the drawing of enough rails for nearly eight miles of railroad, from Wilmington to Andover. This winter, twenty oxen were employed, and as Mr. Richardson was out of health nearly the whole concern came under my supervision. Several of the same men were engaged on this work that were employed on Pemberton Hill and Cedar Swamp, *viz*: — Horace Emmons, Jacob Morey, Abijah Richardson, William Goodhue, and William Badger.

Some of these men had been employed as teamsters seven years, and Horace Emmons, although an excellent teamster, was fond to be worth more to oversee men than oxen. I first hired him 1832, at the commencement of the work on the Boston and Lowell Railroad, for $11 per month, and he never asked me to raise his wages, but only said he was willing to continue work and I might give him what he earned. His wages were gradually raised from time to time, till for the last month I paid him $52, and would gladly have hired him longer at the same price.

Young men, in this glass you may see the reward of faithfulness in another man's employ. Always be true to your employer. "Once a rogue and always mistrusted," is an old and true proverb. Remember money should be earned before it is received, and you should study the best interest of your employer instead of studying how you can get the most money out of him.

I do not think that there has been a Spring since I attended the Agricultural Meetings at the State House, but what I have had applications for an overseer on a farm, where he could obtain $500 per year, and have been really sorry when casting an eye back on the men I have employed to find "unblemished timber" so scarce. One other hand, whose faithful services I must not overlook, was Isaac Damon, who worked for me more than two years, and such was my confidence in his integrity, that I would willingly trust him with "untold gold."

I sometimes hear young men say that they can get nothing to do. If you cannot get the price you want, you had better work for smaller wages than cultivate idleness. If those who have work to do will not employ you, be assured that there is a "leak in the bucket," and you must search out the leak and stop it up, and thus make your services acceptable.

When I had decided on one of those reliable men, and applied to him, I generally found him so engaged that he did not wish to leave.

Let it not be inferred from what has been said, that I have not had many good men, yes, very good, in my employ not named; but before I can recommend a man to take charge of a farm, "I must summer and winter him;" I must know his habits of tending stock as well as his skill in cultivating land.

It is my wish that young men would hereby be encouraged to be faithful to their employers. When that fact is fully established, it is a firm stepping-stone to prosperity. Faithfulness to trust is pecuniarily as well as morally the best policy.

Before closing I must mention the pleasant winters I have enjoyed in the Legislature of my native State, listening to speeches and debates clothed with the wisdom and experience of the honorable of our times.

The winters of 1841 and of 1857, were spent in that agreeable, and I trust profitable situation.

If ever I benefited the Commonwealth, in which it is my privilege to dwell, it was during my second term as Representative. A bill was pending before the House, called the "Usury Bill;" this bill I considered unjust, and labored with all the honest ingenuity and skill I was master of to bring about its defeat. I endeavored to state facts before the House, showing that the passage of this bill would bring ruin on many of the most enterprising farmers in Massachusetts, and I have the consolation of knowing that it was defeated. After the adjournment, many of the members came to me, saying that they were heartily glad to hear my speech, for it had brought many things to their minds of which they never thought before, and that they certainly should have voted for the bill had it not been for the ideas gained from it. Reader, the same spirit that prompts men to say, "Slavery is a blessing," will always be trying to get such bills passed, and I wish you to take into serious consideration the effect this bill would have upon the community.

First — It would open the door for the capitalist to take more advantage than he ever yet had in his power; and we know from experience that this power is always exercised under the pressure of the hardest times. The greater the cry that money is scarce, the more there is lying idle. We have seen enough of human nature to know that man will take all the interest he can get under cover of law. Remove this law and what disastrous consequences follow. How many enterprising young men there are in this State, that have bought farms, paid half the purchase money and given a mortgage on the farm for security for the remainder, honestly expecting to pay but six per cent interest. How long would it be before they must pay twelve per cent, if such a bill passed? Then how long would it be before real estate would fall one-half in value? And then what an amount of farms would fall into the hands of land-sharks.

Take another illustration. A merchant has goods in his store to the amount of from one thousand to five thousand dollars, on which he wishes to make an honest living and interest on his money, and this is right. Now this must come out of the consumer, and generally out of that valuable class of citizens who work for their daily bread. I know that there are many who say if there were no bounds to interest, money would be easier and plentier. Of course I do not believe them; they are the very class who wish to let money.

In short, to increase the per cent of interest, serves to make rich men richer, and poor men poorer; and whoever brings it about, brings a curse upon the community.

Farmers and mechanics — God has put in your power to prevent usury ever running higher than 6 per cent. Look to it that you use that power. Never, never, cast your vote for a man who would oppress the poor to fill the coffers of the rich.

At another time when a bill for a horse railroad was before the House, and much opposition raised on account of obstructing the streets, I pondered the subject and was determined to collect facts that would show how horse cars would compare with omnibuses, and horses and chaises. I found an omnibus to average twelve to the load. I then stood on Cambridge bridge till sixteen chaises passed and found they averaged one and one-half, making in all twenty-four. I then went to several Conductors of horse cars and ascertained their average to be twenty-four each way for a month. By this I found that eight horses with two omnibuses had to pass through the streets to convey the same number of passengers that two horses and one car would carry, and sixteen horses and sixteen chaises to carry the same number.

These facts I stated. And further stated, that when the grant was made to the public from the landowners, it was not specified what they should travel upon, whether gravel or stone, wood or iron. Therefore the public have a right to take their choice and travel how, or in what vehicles they please.

I know the rails are some inconvenience to travelers, but reader when you can find a safer or better way than horse cars, then you may go against them. The bill passed the House.

One word on choosing Representatives for Town or State, as the trust is of vast importance.

Make choice of men possessed of good natural sense, in the common acceptation of that term, but who have been for the most part employed in agriculture; or more properly in the business the all-wise Creator first designed for man "To dress the garden and keep it." No occupation is so well calculated to improve the mind and morals, as farming. Not an hour passes while cultivating the soil, but one is reminded of his dependence on our beneficent Creator, and our obligations to imitate Him "who maketh his sun to rise on the evil and on the good, and sendeth rain on the just and on the unjust."

Men whose profession it is to make a lie appear like the truth, and who like Southern slaveholders, have been bred to the degrading idea that it is right to oppress the poor to help the rich, should be avoided, as we would avoid enlisting under a taskmaster for life.

Laboring men, farmers and mechanics are the men to make the laws for themselves. For certainly they compose the greater part of our population. Then choose your officers for Town and County from that class, and be active to bring about such a choice. If we mean to maintain a Free Government and avoid in future the horrors of civil war, we must elect men to rule us who are determined to discharge their duty to God and their country without fear of men or devils.

While serving in the capacity of Representative, I was introduced to the Agricultural Meetings at the State House. They are generally held weekly when the Legislature is in session, when different topics of agriculture are discussed, and it has been my privilege to attend them occasionally for twenty-one years, much to my satisfaction. I have often heard the remark by men who never attended one of these meetings in their lives, that they are good for nothing. To those I would say, if you cannot profit by hearing such men as Marshall P. Wilder, Dr. Loring, Sanford Howard, Leander Witherell, John W. Procter, Josiah Quincy, Jr., Elijah Wood, Jr., John Brooks, Wm. Buckminster and Simon Brown, and many more I could mention, relate their knowledge and experience in cattle, horses, hogs and sheep, on cultivating the soil with everything it produces, on fruit trees of all kinds, farming implements, manure, and everything appertaining to agriculture, you may set it down that you are a dull scholar, and had better never try to get your living by farming. For my own part, I feel under obligations to those Honorable gentlemen, for the instructions received from them, and for the last ten years I have turned my attention more particularly to farming, dairy-work and stock-raising.

❖ SECOND ARRANGEMENT ❖

STONE WORK

In the year 1809, passing through 'Squire William Blanchard's farm, I observed his three men laying stone wall, Charles Burt being foreman. I noticed he tried a stone several ways, and then about to throw it aside in a pet, said, "It won't lay no way."

"Hold on, Burt," said I, "There is one way that stone will lay and make good work."

"I should like to know which way?"

Putting my hand to the stone, I said, "make that the bed and lay it over the joint of those two."

He did so, and it made solid work without a pinner. The 'Squire stood by, puffing a cigar, and said, "Young man what shall I give you to work for me three hours?" This was the first time I had ever spoken with him.

"One shilling per hour," said I, having no idea he would give it, eight cents being the common price.

"Now," said he, "I want you to pick out every stone and direct how it shall be laid, and I will give you your price."

An hour or so afterwards, the 'Squire appeared again with something to cheer the hands and quench thirst.

"Burt, how do you get along?" said he.

"Faster than we have done, and easier too," said Burt.

Again the 'Squire came, saying, "Young man, your three hours are out; walk up to the house and I will pay you; but you must stop and take a cup of tea with me and my wife first."

At that time I should rather "take a licking," as boys say, than sit down to tea with them; but I soon found myself introduced to the most amiable and social of women. And since that time I never regretted my acquaintance with the Blanchard family. To this time, whenever opportunity offers, I can spend an hour very agreeably with any of the descendants of that couple. After this occurrence whenever there was a culvert to be built in the highway, Sheldon was called on to take charge of it.

The first year of my residence on the Flint farm built a stone wall around his family graveyard, near his house. He wished a permanent wall, that would stand the lapse of centuries, as he might leave his farm. I made inquiries in that respect a few days since, and was informed that not a stone had fallen from its place, neither from the graveyard or hog-sty wall that I built. People had told him, no man could lay a wall that hogs would not throw down. So well pleased was he that no other man was employed to lay stone for him while I occupied his farm, a period of thirteen years.

During the first year of my railroad experience, when Deacon Addison Flint had charge of the stone work, and I of the earth, as I chanced to be looking at the stone layers, they turned an uncouth stone weighing more than three tons round and round, and were about casting it aside when I ventured to say, "Hold on, I can see a way for it."

"How is that?" said the foreman.

I told them, and the trial satisfied all parties. John Haggins, Dept. Engineer, being present, soon brought about an exchange. Flint was put on the earth, and I upon the stonework.

I wish to avoid the imputation of egotism in saying that my abutments of bridges stood so well that I have since been employed to rebuild abutments to bridges built by others, on the Boston and Lowell Railroad, to the number of fourteen.

    1. Where the cars run under the road leading from
        Medford to East Cambridge.

2. The arched bridge at Somerville Station.

3. The next bridge North of that.

4. The Willow bridge, where the cattle are now taken off.

5. The arched bridge under the railroad over Medford river, spanning about fifty feet.

6. The bridge under the road leading from Symmes' Corner to Winchester West side.

7. The bridge at the river near the same place.

8. Under the railroad in Parker's Mill-pond.

9. The bridge near East Woburn and Stoneham Station.

10. The Boutelle bridge so-called.

11. The Saw-pit Woods bridge.

12. Kendall bridge in Billerica.

13. Tufts bridge in Billerica.

14. Bridge over the road leading from Billerica to Tewksbury.

During all this reconstruction of bridges, the business was so managed that the cars were never delayed one moment, much to the gratification of the Agents.

For Patrick T. Jackson, Charles S. Storrow, Waldo Higginson, William Parker, Agents, and Benjamin. F. Baldwin, Engineer, I have done work to the amount of over $100,000. And all this without any written contract, neither of us being bound by writing, and I ever found their memorandum of the agreement proved as strong as any bond could make it. I thank God that he has raised up these honest, fair-dealing, upright men. But to my sorrow, on one other railroad I found both Engineer and Agents to be men of a very different character.

I was once invited to take the job of constructing several miles of railroad in company with two others. I had about concluded to engage, when one of them said to me, "If you do take the stone work, I don't want you should do it as you did the Boston and Lowell, to stand forever, but get it done as cheap as we can and get it accepted, and secure our pay for it, and then I don't care if it all goes to destruction the next day."

"Then I will have nothing to do with it," said I, "for I have never yet laid a stone on the railroad that I thought likely to endanger any man's life and I never mean to."

The road was built, and soon after I heard of the stonework giving way, the engine falling through, bringing one man to a most excruciating death.

In the year 1839, I was employed in making an abutment for the Boston and Maine road, at the bridge over the Merrimac river on the Bradford side. I likewise teamed rails and ties for nine miles of road, of which a man named Clark was agent. He told me in the commencement that they, the Company, had no right to the land; I must beg my way along as well as I could. And sure I did have to beg my way. One amusing circumstance I will relate. As we approached land belonging to a middle-aged widow, in depositing our rails, the neighbors mustered their heavy teams and built a wall across the track completely blocking up our way. I informed Clark of the circumstance when he gave orders to have the wall taken out of the way. Jacob Morey's team was the first to start on to forbidden ground. Just as he started I espied a woman hurrying across the field toward us, who proved to be the rightful owner of the land.

Some hundreds had collected to see the "fight," as they termed it. To Morey I said, "Don't stop for any man, but be sure not drive over a woman."

She did not happen to be quick enough to get ahead of the oxen, and so ran in between the off ox and the load. This chanced to be the worst ox to kick I ever owned; I should not have dared to stand there myself. I hastened to the spot with all eagerness and warned the woman of her danger, but I presume she did not believe one word I told her. That he did not kick was truly a wonder, but he stood passive as a lamb. On looking round I saw that her son had placed a long wagon crosswise ahead of the other teams and blockaded them. A hand was dispatched to get some hay for Morey's team, with orders for the other teamsters to do the same, "for if we must stand here, they must have something to eat," I said.

It being the month of March, it was all mud and water where she stood. I then brought a plank and laid it carefully in for her to stand upon, saying, "If you will stand there, I will make you as comfortable as I can." I was just as sociable as lay in my power, but not a word could I get out of her, or a smile from her lips until 'Squire Tilton from Exeter, then treasurer of the railroad, said, "Sheldon, I have always heard that you were a smart man; I am surprised that you let one woman stop all this work. Why don't you drive over her?"

"'Squire," said I, "for more than twenty years I have not been in the habit of driving more than half way over so handsome a woman as that."

This brought a smile to her face and loosened her tongue.

"How long are you going to keep your oxen here?" asked she.

"If I can't go ahead I shall keep my cattle here till twelve o'clock Saturday night, and bring them back Sunday night at twelve o'clock; and as I have not engaged to board anywhere, should like to board with you. Now if you will go up and get supper I will come and help you eat it. What time do you have supper?"

"We eat our supper at six o'clock," said she.

She then stepped out, and I helped her up the bank with what politeness I was master of, and for once I must say I was glad to see one of the fair sex walking from me. She had stood there at least half an hour.

When six o'clock came, I made my way up to the house,

entered without rapping as if it had been my boardinghouse. I found all seated at table but one who waited and
was detained. I took the chair appropriated to her, and
said, "I suppose this chair is reserved for me."

"If you are determined you will eat supper with us, you
may sit in that chair."

"Madam, I am not only determined to eat supper with
you, but I am determined to board with you while my work
continues in this neighborhood."

While eating she asked, "Do you intend to keep those
teams where my son is, as long as you proposed to keep the
other team?"

"Yes, certainly I do."

"Then I will send for him to drive his team home."

We grew quite sociable before supper was finished, and
could talk about the railroad pleasantly. She asked me,
"Was that a real kicking ox of yours, or did you say so to
frighten and drive me away?"

"Oh, it was a real kicking ox; and it is an astonishment to
me that he did not kick you under the wheels."

I boarded with her as long as I pleased, and found it a
good boarding place.

After the consummation of this job the same company
advertised for proposals for laying nine miles of rails, and
eight miles of stonework. I, with five others, carried in
proposals for the rail-work, and I by myself carried in
proposals for the stonework. The Directors voted to accept
of both, and we met to make the contracts. The contract for
the rail-work was made, but Bailey's name stood first, although mine was first on the proposal. This done, 'Squire
Clark, the agent, wished to see me alone. When by ourselves, he said, "I wish to say to you in confidence, I don't
know how far we shall go with our road, or when we shall
be obliged to stop. I don't want to make any contract for the
stonework, but I want you to go there and work when I say
so, and do as I say, and I will see you well paid for it."

After a while, Haywood, the Engineer, came and said to

me, "How soon can you be at Exeter, ready to work at Capt. Fernald's bridge?"

"How soon do you want me if I could be there?"

"I want you to be there very much tomorrow morning at eight o'clock."

"I think I can be there at that time," I replied.

We loaded our stone tools and set out at midnight; travelled fourteen miles before sunrise; stopped and breakfasted at Dodge's tavern, and proceeded to the ground and were ready there at eight o'clock.

While waiting, I put up four stakes at the four corners where I judged the bridge ought to be. At nine o'clock, Haywood and Clark arrived.

"Mr. Haywood, where shall I put in this bridge?" I asked.

"Where do you think it best to put it in?" said he.

"Where those four stakes stand."

"Then put it there," said he.

"I don't know whether you will or not," said an unknown gentleman.

"Is this Capt. Fernald?" said Mr. Haywood.

"Fernald is my name," he answered.

"I am very happy to see you, Capt. Fernald," said Haywood.

The parties, after talking together a few minutes, told me that I might go to work.

A number of walls meeting here, just where I wanted to work, I asked, "Who owns these walls?"

"I own them," said F.

"These walls will serve for backers, I would like to buy them. What will you take for them?"

"Thirty dollars," said the Captain.

"Captain Fernald, they are not worth $10 for you to move away."

He started quick, a characteristic of a sea captain. "It is nothing to you what they are worth to me; if I sell them to you I want what they are worth to you."

"Capt. Fernald, if you will allow me to make remarks five minutes, I will then hear you an hour if you wish me to. We will suppose these stones to be worth $30 to me, but only $10 to you, would it not be more just to divide and call it $20, giving me $10 and you $10, than it would be to take either extreme?"

"You have convinced me; you shall have them for $20. You and I are friends now." And pointing to two lots of land, he said, "I own that land and if you want any stone there, you are welcome to get them."

This bridge was finished without any special trouble, and about ten rods further up we put in an abutment on Fernald's land, close to the line, intending to build another on the other side, owned by a man named Swasey, to accommodate both in their farm operations. I had no acquaintance with Swasey but hoped to get along without difficulty. The morning came and we started as usual to commence our work. I saw a man coming across the field with a gun in his hand, and when he came up, he said, "What are you going to do here?"

"I am going to dig away and put in a abutment on this side for a bridge to accommodate Capt. Fernald and Mr. Swasey."

"I will put a ball through the heart of the first man who takes a stone from this wall."

I saw there was a dead set, and turning to the stone layers, said, "Go up into Judge Smith's pasture to splitting stone; I have bought the privilege of taking out all the stone I wished. And you teamsters, go and draw them and lay them on the highway, handy to be used, if we are ever allowed to do the work."

My boarding place was Dodge's tavern, where Swasey made his appearance every evening and held converse with me. It soon become apparent that he was smoothing down, and in about a week he said to me, "Mr. Sheldon, we think about here that you know more concerning railroads than we do, and some think that you will say just what you think about it. Now tell me, had I better let the road pass through my land or not."

"Certainly, you had," said I. "You told me the other night that you had three thousand cords of standing wood, and as soon as the railroad is in operation, every cord of that wood will be worth fifty cents more than it now is. They are now buying wood at Wilmington for $3 per cord, to run their engine to East Kingston; and as soon as the cars run wood will be worth as much here as it is in Wilmington. The cut is already made through your farm, and if you could stop the work from going further, you could never get one cent of damages; and I advise you to take stock in the road for damages."

"When do you want to go to work on that abutment, if I would let you?"

"Tomorrow morning at sunrise," said I.

"Then you may go on," he replied.

We were on the work at sunrise, and soon Mr. Swasey made his appearance with his team. His first question was, "Where shall I begin to work?" I told him, and he worked all day like a hero, as he was, and at night he pulled off his hat and, bowing low, said, "You are welcome to this day's work, because you would not be mad even though I threatened your life. Sheldon, when I came out here with my gun, it was loaded with two balls, and I certainly should have put them through your heart had you attempted to move a stone."

Pretty much after this fashion we worked our way along through all this section. Sometimes we were not able to lay a stone for a week, being obliged to move back and forth and work a few days in a place when and where we could get a chance. When we could get no opportunity to lay stone we employed ourselves in getting them out and drawing them near where we hoped to lay them. These delays certainly impeded the work more than thirty-three per cent, or nearly one-half; and besides the workmen began to grow uneasy and fretful at moving about so much and not being able to show more for their work.

One day I met the agent and engineer in a sleigh on Kingston plain. "Clark," said I, "hadn't we better leave the work and go home, for certainly some days we do not earn twenty-five cents where we spend a dollar."

"Haven't I said to you times enough, stay there and do what I want you to, and I will see you well paid. Don't say anything more to me about leaving unless I tell you to."

So poor was the credit of the corporation at that time, that not a stick of timber could be bought for a temporary bridge, unless Edward Crane or I would promise to see it paid for. Crane was on the earth and I on the stonework; we were the only two undertakers on the ground.

As a palliation for the seeming insanity that prevailed among the land owners, I would say that there was a prevailing belief that the road would never be finished. The stock was as low as sixty per cent., and they feared they would not get damages.

When the work was all completed, they owed me $8,500 as honestly as ever one man owed another. I sent an order to the Treasurer for $45 and he refused to pay it, saying he owed me nothing.

When it was announced that the Corporation "owed me nothing," there were forty writs levied upon my property within twenty-four hours, for the announcement was made in the long entry of the largest hotel in Exeter. In this situation, the reader can well judge what a waste was made of my property. One instance I will here mention. About a fortnight prior to this there was a large sale of chestnut timber in New Hampshire, at auction. I attended and bought $1650 worth; paid $150 cash and gave three notes of $500 each, one to be paid in six months, one in one year and one in eighteen months. In a few days a large timber dealer offered me $500 for the bargain. Knowing it was the best bargain of timber I ever bought in my life, and wanting winter work for my oxen and men, I thought it not wise to accept the offer, not doubting but that I should receive my pay for that job and could handle it to my liking and turn it at last to more advantage. The money being withheld, and all my property attached, I lost not only the bargain but the $150 previously paid. The man who offered me $500 for the bargain, afterwards bought the lot, and I have been informed by good authority that he cleared $3,000 on the bargain. Great numbers of chestnut ties, from this lot, were carried on the railroad to Boston and then shipped to R.

Hon. Thomas West succeeded Mr. Clark in office, and became agent of the road. I made him the offer to leave the case to three men, who were directors of the road when the work was done. This was not accepted. I then offered to leave it to Patrick T. Jackson, James F. Baldwin and Chas. S. Storrow. This offer did not meet their approbation. I then commenced a suit against them. After several months I received a communication by letter to meet the Directors at Dover on a specified day. On arriving at Andover, I was introduced to one of the Directors by the name of Weld. On the way, we talked over the matter, and he said he had understood that I had once offered to leave it to three men who were directors on the road when the work was done.

"I did," said I.

"Will you renew that offer?" he asked.

"I will," was my answer.

When we arrived at Haverhill, Mr. West came into the cars, and Mr. Weld related the conversation that had taken place between us on the road, and expressed his surprise that the corporation should suffer themselves to be sued when I had made them so fair an offer.

"I don't know," said Mr. West, "but he has made them an offer that they would rather accept of than that. I believe he has offered to leave it to Jackson, Baldwin and Storrow."

"I did make that offer."

"Will you renew it?" said Mr. Weld.

"I will renew both offers, and you may take your choice."

"It shall be done; it shall be settled without going further in court."

On going into the room with the Directors, they said that there was nothing in the way of settlement; if I would retire, Mr. West and I could talk it over in the cars on our way home. When the subject was introduced, Mr. West said, "The Directors all meet at Boston tomorrow. If you will come and bring your bill, and we do not pay it, Jackson, Baldwin and Storrow shall settle it."

To Boston I went, and met West in State street, when he accosted me thus, "Sheldon, they will not have Jackson on this reference at any rate."

"You have already agreed to have him," said I.

"Well go in and see what they say."

When in, it was soon announced that Mr. Jackson could not be allowed to serve as referee.

"Gentlemen," I said, "if you will give me any reason why Mr. Jackson cannot be admitted to serve, I will be content with another man."

"Sheldon," said Mr. Weld, "we find, here in Boston, that you have done so much work for Mr. Jackson, and have been with him so much that he will believe every word you say, and we may as well leave the case to him."

My answer was, "It is no disgrace to me after being with him, and doing as much for him as I have done, to have him believe all I say."

The chairman then said, "Name a man living somewhere between Boston and Dover, within three miles of our road."

I then named twenty men, all of whom were rejected as soon as named. "Gentlemen," said I, "it is of no use for me to pick out a man; name one yourselves."

"Col. Duncan, of Haverhill," said Mr. Weld.

"I do not want a better man," said I, "he is one of the first three that I offered to leave it to."

As the cars were about to leave, they decided that John Flint, of Andover, should write notices to the several gentlemen, and I should see that they had them.

So early was I up the next morning that I travelled eight miles before John Flint was out of bed. He wrote the notices and I flew up and down on the railroad and carried them to the respective gentlemen that same day. But strange to believe, before the specified day came, I received a letter from Duncan that they would have neither of the Boston gentlemen at any rate to sit on the case between me and the Corporation.

Here the case hung until Col. Duncan was appointed Auditor by the Court. He appointed a meeting at Andover, to which the several parties repaired. After Mr. Haywood's testimony, Mr. West advanced a proposal to give me $7000 if I would take $1000 in their railroad stock. After a little deliberation I decided to accept it, for this reason. The bargain was made privately between me and Mr. Clark, on that account I had no evidence of it and Mr. Haywood said on the stand, he could not recollect the conversation between Clark and me on Kingston Plain. Furthermore, the same gentleman came to me and said the stone work referred to as a sample for me was not good enough but was filing, and asked what way it could be made better. I informed him by splitting out the stone with wedges instead of powder, but it would cost more. He asked, "How much more?"

"One dollar per yard," was the answer.

"Well," said he, "get them out with wedges."

On the stand he acknowledged the work was $1 per yard better, but he *could–not–recollect* ever giving any order for that course.

About three years after commencing my suit, when I received from the Corporation $7000, I made the best settlement with creditors circumstances would permit, and began life again with only $75.

I would like to say distinctly to every Stockholder of the Boston and Maine Road, that when your Corporation was in a sinking condition I did what I could to further on the work, day and night, some nights going without any sleep. And now knowing how I have been treated, are there not some lovers of justice among you who are willing to make some recompense in view of the faithfulness with which I have serve you. Some may say, why did you risk so much without a written contract? I would state in reply, I had done more than $100,000 worth of work for men who were agents, and always found their word to be good as their bond; this gave me too much confidence in men.

To Mr. West I would say, you have had a long time to reflect, that you once agreed to let Jackson, Baldwin and Storrow settle the case between me and your Corporation. Then you refused to let Mr. Jackson act, and Col. Duncan's name was substituted in his stead. The next thing, you refused to let Mr. Baldwin and Mr. Storrow act. By so doing I consider you ruined a man who had served your Corporation faithfully. After so long a time if you have repented of what I consider a great sin, I trust you will set about making some recompense. But if your heart is yet hardened, I pray God, when your eyes are closed in death, to have mercy on your soul.

A job of stonework at Nashua, N. H., next claims attention. I was called by the Directors of the Nashua and Lowell Road to look at a piece of work considered difficult to do, and keep the cars running. Here the cars ran across Indian Head canal and then followed its bank, partly over the water, about five hundred feet. It was supported by piles nineteen feet above the bottom of the canal. These had begun to decay and it was found necessary to reconstruct the road. The first thing was to build two abutments near the depot, fifty-five feet long and nineteen feet high, with a pier in the center of the same length; then a wall three hundred feet long of the same height, five feet below the surface of the water. Then there were four arches to turn. Around these we built a coffer dam, that we might prosecute the work without water. They spanned twenty feet each, making eighty feet. They were to carry off surplus water in case of a freshet. The piles and wood-work were all taken away, and this large job of stonework done without hindering the cars one minute.

Gratitude forbids that I should pass unnoticed a narrow escape there. One of the workmen desired a staging built outside the wall over the canal.

"Build it so strong," said I, "that two men can stand upon it and lift with all their strength with a crowbar."

It was used in that way two days. On the third morning the applicant desired me to go on to the staging to look at a large stone laid the night before. I descended with some caution, I hardly know why, keeping hold of the stones all the time, but alas, the instant I let go, and stood on the staging, down came the whole concern and I was precipitated backwards into the canal, which that day received the whole water of Nashua river, for the purpose of having a dam repaired, and making the current in the canal very swift. This occurred near the guard-gates, through which I knew I must go, and feared I should lodge on some timber, but thanks to Morey I went through safe. One of my men, Harvey Putnam, hearing the crash of the staging, run to the place, and saw nothing but the broken staging in the canal and my hat on the top of the water. He then ran below the gates and could discern a shirt sleeve in the foam. Determined to help what he could, he descended the wall, laid in steps, and hanging on by the stones with his hand, stretched his legs into the water, calling out, "Get hold of my legs." I was tumbling over in the dashing water, but heard him distinctly, and reaching about with all my might, luckily caught hold of a boot and held on until helped out of the water. I repaired to the scene of danger as soon as the case would permit, and found that a small strip of cast iron had taken the place of an iron crowbar that supported the staging. Feeling confident that the whole affair was designed, I took the small piece remaining in the wall, where it had been broken off, my workmen being gathered around, and stepped toward the suspected man, holding the iron directly before his face, neither of us speaking a word. His countenance turned very pale, and strange as the fact may seem, within an hour proposed to leave the work. I am fully satisfied from the circumstances, that the man who kept the Time Book, hired him to do the trick, by ordering $15 to be paid him out of the Corporation's money. That they designed to take my life, I have no doubt; and if, while I live, that man should be sick and likely to die, I will go to him, if I can, and ask him if the time-keeper hired him to exchange the crowbar for that piece of cast iron, and get me on the stage for the purpose of destroying my life. In the beginning, I was cautioned by a man intimately acquainted with this time-keeper, to look out for him, stating that he was an artful man, and that when the job was well under way it would be like him to take hold of it himself, if he could by any means get rid of me, and then say, "Sheldon began the job but could not finish it."

I have had the superintendence of building or rebuilding the abutments of eighteen bridges on the Boston and Lowell road, and many culverts. And on the Boston and Maine road I have built abutments for eight bridges, besides numerous culverts and cow-guards. On the South Reading Branch I have likewise laid abutments to eight bridges and turned an arch over the river that divides Essex from Middlesex County, together with many cow-guards and culverts on the same road, and also at Bradford, at Ward Hill, where the road runs near Merrimac river.

Slocum, of Haverhill, and myself had been engaged in a winter's work of drawing lumber to Maine railroad in Kingston. We then hired an engine, engineer, train of cars and fireman, to take it down to Andover Saw Mills. I was conductor and espied a crack running lengthwise of the ties, about the middle of the road fifty-five feet in length. This was in the beginning of Spring. I made signal to stop when fairly over it, and in less than five minutes it all slid down into the river. As we stood gazing, the road-master came up, and in surprise and almost crazed, freshets were rising so fast, said, "Sheldon, you can think faster than I can, for heaven's sake tell me what to do?"

"Send a man," said I, "as fast as he can go to North Andover, to tell the conductor to turn his engine behind and back up here; and you must have my engine to bring the passengers from Haverhill up, and they must walk over and change cars."

He then remarked, "You must mend up this place as soon as possible, for I have as much as I can attend to elsewhere; our road is going to pieces."

The fourteen men with me were speedily set to work throwing stones into the hole, for there were lots of them near by on the opposite side. I then sent a man with the engine down to Haverhill to tell Slocum to send dinner for fourteen men, and all the men he could raise. They brought dinner and a passenger train together, and by mustering neighbors we swelled our force to forty-three men and six oxen.

At that time, as good luck would have it, the moon's clear light enabled us to continue our work through the night. Burrill, the Agent for running the cars, came up with the supper, looked on, and said, "Sheldon, how many days before the cars can run here?"

"I want you to bring up a good second supper for twenty-three hungry men," said I, "and then I can tell you better about it. Bring it as late as you like to sit up to accommodate us."

The supper came about 11 o'clock, and it was as good a supper as men ever need to eat. It may be called second supper, or night dinner, for well do I know from experience that a man while laboring needs food as much at night as in day. Six hours labor is quite enough for any man between meals.

The embankment that gave way was fifty-five feet in length and fifteen feet below the rail, but the ties kept their place, being frozen in on the opposite side, only half the track going down. When supper came, Burrill asked me, "Can you tell now how many days it will be before the cars can run?"

"If you don't hear from me before the sun rises, you may start your cars along as though nothing had occurred."

"Sheldon, are you crazy?" said he.

"No, I hope not; but you may start on the cars, telling them to proceed with caution when they approach this place."

The cars did come at the usual time, and I stopped to see them safely over and then went back to Haverhill to breakfast.

The secret of accomplishing this great work in so short a time, was just this: we threw the stones in and allowed them to find their own bed, and when they had gone as far as they could, they would lay there till moved by other power. There were plenty of stones here that had been taken from the ledge that we wanted to get off the line of the railroad. When we had filled within six feet of the rails, we placed the stones in a wall directly under them, throwing others down both sides, thus making the work substantial.

After this job was completed and the road had been used some days, Charles Storrow, then a director on the road, said, "Had that happened on the Boston and Lowell road and been repaired in the usual way, it would have cost the corporation more than $1000," but the whole expense here was only $53."

Another witness. Onslow Stearns, agent for building the

Northern road, once said to me, "Sheldon, your filling up that hole at Ward Hill, as you did, has saved the Northern Railroad Co. many thousand dollars, through their adopting the same plan.

Were this mode of building embankments adopted, where stone is plenty, it would be found a labor-saving operation above the old fashioned, perpendicular wall, where sometimes many feet must be laid in mud and water, a most repulsive work.

Reader, remember this night's work was done for the corporation whose agent afterwards ruined me.

I went to Brookline to build a County road over half a mile of marsh and another half a mile through orchards, gardens and strawberry beds, and then through a piece of reclaimed swamp where English grass was mowed. The road was an expensive one, and the greatest saving in calculation, in the whole job, was in laying a strip of marsh grass each side of the road and raking it in for the horses to travel on while carting on the first gravel. After the road was completed over the reclaimed swamp, and we had passed over it with heavy loads for several days, down went about ten rods of it out of sight, and at once water flowed over to the depth of thirty-five feet. To buy the gravel and fill up this enormous mouth was quite an expense, but as I took the job by the yard it only made more work for us.

Whenever I think of the committee who engaged me to do this work, it brings to mind what Christ said to his disciples, "Have not I chosen you twelve and one of you is a devil." I firmly believe the treasurer and committee, save one, to be true, Christian men, and likewise, judging from the Scripture, "A tree is known by its fruits," many of the neighbors to whom I was sometimes indebted.

In the month of February, 1856, I was visited with the severest fit of sickness I ever suffered. I was first attacked with pleurisy; that increased so fast that my family, anxious for my safety, sent the next day for Dr. Edmund F.

Kittredge, of New Ipswich, N. H., now of Lowell, Mass. He pronounced the disease Typhoid Pneumonia of a malignant type. The fever ran high; my pulse for several days ranged as high as a hundred and thirty and a hundred and forty. I lost all consciousness from the first, but my faithful family and friends were unremitting in their attention. Nathaniel Parker — mentioned in a former page as among the friends in need — was sure that I could not get well; it would be as great a miracle as any performed in Scripture times. The next week as my wife was watching me and the family were eating dinner, a sudden change, she said, come over my countenance. All left the table in anxious surprise. "Oh," said Parker, with uplifted hands, "he is gone; I told you how it would be."

The doctor, who was present, replied, "He may live to lay cents on your eyes. Rub his extremities quickly, and wet a cloth in hot vinegar and lay it on his stomach as soon as possible." This was at once done, and the breathing improved and the symptoms became better.

He administered some reviving spirit and continued to feed with the same. He remained with me three successive days and nights and soon consciousness began to return. He did not blister or bleed; gave no emetic or physic, yet he carried me through as I believe few others could.

With heartfelt gratitude to Dr. Kittredge I must say, "Under God, to him I owe my life." It was a wonderful mercy in kind Providence that brought him here at my time of greatest need.

"He could not have lived without extra effort," said the doctor. Then never give up friends sick with fever as long as life lasts; no, not even when life is apparently gone. Many, doubtless, pass out of the world that an extra effort would have restored and brought back to life and health again.

Mr. Parker died two years ago.

This Dr. Kittredge is grandson of him who so faithfully watched by me while laid up with the broken leg.

HINTS TO STONE LAYERS

After having so much experience in stone-laying, and after the many tests my work has undergone, I feel confident that no work of mine will fair, unless by some great confusion of nature, or removal by designing hands; and for the benefit of the rising generation, I propose to give some directions to stoneworkers.

TO STONERS OF WELLS—Never, on any account, lay the largest end of the stone in toward the well.

TO FARMERS—Never destroy any part of the strength of your wall for the sake of making it look handsome on a farm. In reality those farm walls always look handsomest that stand best. There has been no better way found to lay farm walls than on large foundation stones, placed on cobbles. In laying a wall on low, frosty ground, where it is necessary to trench, I would recommend to fill the trench with that kind of dry gravel before mentioned for railroad trenches, walks, &c., if it can be had conveniently, or with sand if that cannot be procured. Either of these are better than small stones for two reasons. First, mud will work in among small stones, freeze and heave the wall. Second, it will give more encouragement to the growth of briars and brush than gravel will.

LAYING CULVERTS—Always make the upstream end of the culvert narrower than any other part; this will prevent anything entering it that cannot go through. Always lay the biggest side of the covering stones downward; this will make the joints widest on the top, they will thereby receive a wedge that will not go through.

CELLAR WALL—In laying them always build them plumb. Then the building resting on the top will be in no danger of falling in. To make a good cellar wall a stone should have three good sides, bed, build and face. Back and ends have not much to do either with strength or beauty.

BANK WALL—It is necessary to have one course of stones below the surface, and on the base of the wall, then have the front of the wall placed on the centre of them. Those stones that are placed below the surface need not of necessity, be very large, and it is immaterial of what shape. What is termed cobble stones, the size of a peck measure, will answer a good purpose.

If you want to build your wall five feet high, and have it stand centuries, as I am sure you do, then make the base half the thickness of the height, and barter it on front at least one and one-half inch to the foot. Mind and never put so small stones on the top that a dog running over them will knock them off. If the soil be clay, take it out a few inches wider than the wall and fill in back with good gravel stones, otherwise the clay will run in among the stones, freeze, and heave them, and thus injure the wall.

MILCH COWS

Until recently I have never realized the value of milch cows, and believe but few do realize it as yet. Milk, butter and cheese are not all the benefits we derive from the cow. Every creature that is slaughtered in Eastern markets, gained the first $3 worth on an average from milk. In New York and Massachusetts, there are not less than ten thousand cattle and calves slaughtered, on an average, every week; allowing $3 to each one, (which is a low estimate), the amount is $1,560,000 in one year for these two States alone.

How many varieties can be realized from milk. Nearly all our calfskin leather is produced from milk. Immense quantities of milk are used for food for children, with great economy and propriety. Besides the immense amount of milk, butter and cheese consumed by the human family, not less than fifty pounds of pork can be reckoned on, by

good management, from each cow, arising from sour milk,
buttermilk, whey, &c. Now is it not of the utmost importance that we select the very best cows?

POINTS OF A GOOD MILCH COW—A bright, hazel eye; long,
lean face; wide between the eyes; flat horns, not very large
at the base; pretty large sack, with room for her own dinner; thin hides; small leg bones; large cavity on the front of
the shoulder joint; large milk veins, and milk holes—if you
can find forked milk veins, with two holes on each side, it is
an extra mark, seldom found; well spread bag, running
well forwards; yellow skin; four good sized teats, standing
well apart; two small ones behind called false teats; slim
tail; and as good a sign as any to be found is, open ribs,
with space wide enough between the two last to admit of
three fingers laid in. If the cow is wanted for butter exclusively, the horn should be transparent. This mark I first
received from Mrs. Deacon Parker. Hearing I had an extraordinary heifer, the good old lady came over to see it.
While walking in front of the stall, she exclaimed, "Here is
a heifer that will make a good cow, I care nothing about
your father's great heifers."

"Why," said son Horace, who was showing her around,
"what do you see in that heifer, Mrs. Parker, to admire?"

"Why her horns are all butter," said she. "I have taken
care of a dairy more than fifty years, and I never knew it to
fail."

In fact that was the very heifer she came to see. I have
noted it ever since and found it so. Mrs. Parker was considered an extraordinary dairy woman; her butter, as well
as that of her daughter Buck, always commanding the
highest market price.

To purchasers I would say, whenever you find these
marks, you need to inquire what breed she is of; you will be
sure to get a good cow.

With regard to color, I prefer light red or brindle, because
they descended from the Black Spanish, and Denmark cat-

tle, imported into Dover nearly two hundred years ago. From them I think sprang the best race of dairy stock this country has ever been in possession of. Still I would not reject a cow on account of color, if she possessed the marks before mentioned.

From experience I feel safe in saying that a woman who is a good manager would, from the products of two good cows well kept, maintain the year round, a family of four, say herself, husband, and two children, and pay a reasonable tax on the cows, pasture and home-lot. If her husband pay the expense of keeping the cows, it would be all required for the maintenance of his family. This will apply to any location within fifteen miles of Boston.

In looking over the utility of animals, I am constrained to say, if we could have but one kind of animals, cow, horse, sheep or hog, the cow must be preferred.

OXEN

SIGNS OF A GOOD WORKING OX—Bright hazel eye, which denotes intellect, or a disposition to receive instruction, and a readiness to obey it; lean, long head; broad between the eyes; wide, open nostrils; horns not more than medium size at the base — these show an ox keen to pull and one that can endure the heat of the day; straight knees, toes pointing straight forward — these show that the ox can travel on pavement, or hard, frozen ground; full bosom; round in the chest; last ribs projecting out as large as the hip bones; straight on the back; small tail; wide across the gambrel; large cord at the gambrel — these last mentioned marks denote strength and constitution; when he stands his hind feet should be well in under him — this shows his limbs were made to carry his body, and will carry it easily.

Short heads will start quick at the whip but soon forget it — generally eye servants; horns large at the base, with small nostrils, is not likely to work well in a hot day; black eyes and black nose, inclined to both kick and run away; picked toes and turning out, crooked knees and turning together, cannot travel on hard roads; the toes turning out brings the strain upon the inside claws, which long continued, produces lameness at the joint between the hoof and hair, or what is called ring-bone; if his hind legs are too far behind him, it denotes laziness; if the ribs drop down flat, not being so wide through the ribs as through the hip bones, he has no great constitution.

It is said, "There are exceptions to general rules," but these signs may generally be relied upon.

While walking near Quincy Market, Boston, one day, I met a man who invited me to go with him, which I did. He purchased a nice turkey and presented it to me, saying "Accept this as a token of gratitude for the benefits I have derived from practicing your directions for selecting good working oxen. I have practiced them since I first had occasion to buy oxen." Before I could ascertain his name he had disappeared in the crowd.

SHOEING OXEN — The shoe should be broad on the foot, and be set back at the heel about half a inch further than what the foot touches. At the toe, it should not come quite to the end of it. If the toe is very picked, it should not come nearer than about an inch of the end. If the toe be short and broad, it should come almost to the end of the toe.

POINTS OF AN OX FOR TENDER BEEF — Smoky color; long, coarse hair; thin hide, this may be told by pinching it up between the thumb and finger; flat ribs; wide hip bones, quite hollow underneath; then if he be only fat you need not fear, even though he is the worst looking animal you ever put your eye on. These points apply to all horned creatures.

HOW TO SALT BEEF TO KEEP A YEAR — Take four quarts of coarse fine salt, four pounds of brown sugar, one ounce saltpetre, mix well together, to one hundred pounds of beef, packed as solid as it can be; put a board on top of the meat

in the barrel, and a standard to reach from this board to a
timber in the floor overhead; drive in a wedge to keep the
standard tight, and the meat will settle for two or three
days. To prevent the bottom head from bursting out, a
small bit of board should be placed under the barrel within
the chines, before the meat is salted, which should be done
soon after the animal heat is out. No water should be used,
as it takes out the juice of the meat and turns it green and
makes it hard. When a piece is taken out, and the brine
will not cover, put in a small stone and cover the board on
again.

RAISING BULLS

If the object is to raise dairy stock, be sure your bull calf is
from your best dairy cow, and the color of the skin about
the bag should be the same as of a good cow — yellow. A
four teated bull is preferable, but this is rare. My plan is to
raise two bull calves together and break them to yoke quite
small; and I have found that they were worth more than
oxen to plow in my reclaimed swamp when two years old,
as they were light of their strength and could go where
heavy oxen could not. I have likewise found them very use-
ful in carting hay from miry meadows. If a bull will be
worth anything to work, he can be handied easier than a
steer. Some are so stubborn one should never try to handy
them. To put on a light yoke, if you have a good, clear pasture, and let them run in it when six months old, is a good
plan. I once owned a pair that led on a load of wood for four
miles and drew finely, quite as much as I wanted them to,
when only ten months old. I have one of them now. I believe
that a pair of one-year-old bulls will draw as much as a pair
of two-year-old steers. To take a loaded wagon to Concord
Cattle Show, I once put a pair of eighteen months old bulls
to lead, and the teamster thought that they helped as much
as a horse. They certainly do more work according to their

keeping, than steers or oxen. I should not like to keep one older than three years, lest he become cross.

RAISING HEIFER CALVES

It is highly important that heifer calves should be selected from the best cows, but more important is it that their sire should be from the best cow. Do not attempt to raise a heifer calf without first examining her teats. When they are about forty hours old, you may satisfy yourself about their good points, quite as well as at any time before they are two years old, as many of them are about the same as the cows, especially the bag and teats.

Do not keep your calves too high on milk the first summer, because they should be kept up to that standard through the winter. This I deem of great importance and applicable to all kinds of calves; indeed all growing animals should be kept on the advance.

I once took a number of heifer calves, I think ten, to Concord Cattle Show. After the show, Mr. Buckminster, editor of the Massachusetts Ploughman, said in his paper, that he saw a pen of calves labelled, "Native breed; A. G. Sheldon, Wilmington." He observed that the spectators said, "Those calves looked as though the very skimmed milk they were raised on was watered." The spectators were men of excellent judgment, for they were raised on that very article — skimmed milk, indian meal and water. I sold one of these calves, when two years old, for $50, and have frequently heard her owner say that he would not take $100 for her. Some of them that I now know of, cannot be bought for less than $100 each. Seldom does a heifer that is doated upon and fed very high on milk, fully answer the expectation of the owner.

"The size of a bullock depends on the first year." This is an adage that is nearly true. I am fully of opinion that more depends on the first winter than on any other period of the same length in his history. They should have tender hay, some roots, rutabagas or carrots, and oatmeal, which is preferable to any other.

Early calves are preferable for raising to late ones. March calves are decidedly best, yet April will do, but I would not raise one that come in May, unless it was something extraordinary; for this reason, it could not be turned to grass until the feed was tough, and in consequence would not do so well.

ON FEEDING STOCK

It is a great piece of economy in feeding cattle in the barn, to cut all their hay, except the last feeding at night, which should be whole hay. If there be any left in the morning that is fit to eat, I should put it in the cutter and give it to them again. Chopped feed should always be wet, and with hot water if circumstances will permit. Corn stalks are excellent for milch cows whether top stalks or husks; also rutabagas, carrots and parsnips are all good, but I have never been able to determine which is best according to the cost. I think best to sow all of these roots, so that if one kind should not succeed the others might. The more experience I have of pumpkins, the more I am in favor of them; they certainly add to the quantity and to the quality of the butter.

My experience in molasses is, that one half pint given to a good cow will give you four ounces of butter. It should be given in chopped feed by sweetening the water. This is designed solely for chopped feed; when a cow grazes she has no need of it, or anything else, if she has plenty of good grass. Where molasses is used with chopped feed, a little salt should be added.

I endorse the opinion of Hon. Josiah Quincy, Jr., that "a cow is a machine; you can get nothing out of her but what you put into her; but let us remember, the better the machine and the better order it is kept in, the better pay we shall get for running it."

A few apples given occasionally to cows, horses or hogs, are excellent to keep them in a healthy condition. I think a horse would never have botts if he had half a peck of sweet apples once in ten days. Regularity, as it respects time and quantity, is of great importance in feeding all kinds of stock.

Occasional messes to milch cows not only do them no good, but sometimes are decidedly injurious. In the month of June, I once had a bushel of good French turnips chopped and given to five cows that were grazing. The next morning their milk had shrunk down to one half. Surprised at the result, I cast about to understand it. I found the secret in the fact, that the turnips took away their appetite for grass and caused them to wait around for more.

In case of short grazing, cow-corn, as it is commonly called, is very economical, but it should always be given them at night and in the barn, as their appetite will then be good for feed in the morning. To put them in the barn may be thought too much trouble, but I think from experience a cow's extra mess is lost if given anywhere else. It may seem simple, but try the experiment and you will know for yourselves. Common corn is as much better than Virginia corn, as English hay is better than meadow hay, and sweet corn is better than either.

The foregoing hints on calf feeding are designed for locations where milk is worth three cents per quart or more. Those who live far back from the seaboard, where milk is worth but little, are better judges in their own cases than I am.

TO PURCHASERS OF COWS—There may be good cows in every breed among us. Although I am much in favor of native breed, still I would not advise the rejection of a cow on account of her breed if she carries good marks, or give a large price for one on account of her breed without those marks.

TRAINING OXEN AND STEERS

Every steer should have a name. If he has none be sure to give him one the first time he is yoked. Be sure and make each one understand his own name and know when you speak to him; and when you do speak, say just what you mean. Be just as particular in your language with them as you would be with children. When you tell them to haw-to, or gee-off, be sure to make them mind you. Let the word "whoa," or any other word you may choose to substitute, denote "stop," and always make them stop at that, and never use it at any other time. If used at other times they will not know when to stop. A team should stop short at the word "whoa;" and they will, if they never hear it at any other time. Bad results may follow their not being accustomed to do so.

If too lazy or too tired to walk beside your team, never whip them while riding, this will make them haul apart. When your team is moving just as you want to have them, be sure to keep your whip and your tongue perfectly still. When I see a man doing this I know he is more than a middling teamster. Oxen or steers, when going perfectly right, should never be meddled with, any more than boys should be muttered at when they are doing perfectly right.

Always have some particular word to start your team with. My starting word is "come." I always give them notice, and when up to the bow and ready, I speak the word "come," and if either ox does not attend to his business at that word, he is sure to feel the whip. I once knew a man, a good man, and a good farmer, and I presume that he thought he knew how to drive a team as well as any body, but he never handied his off ox. He drove the nigh ox and let the off one go as he pleased. When driving in hay, and when near to the barnyard, he would begin to cry "whoa," "whoa," about as fast as he could speak. I once had the curiosity to count how many times he said it after he arrived at the barnyard bars, and it amounted to one hundred and thirteen times. Still the oxen increased their speed until they got into the barn and were prevented from going further. Doubtless they would have gone in as well if he had not said one word, and stopped as well, because they could not help it. How can an officer command men unless he has a particular word for a particular movement? and how, I wish to know, can we expect oxen to understand better than men?

Steers should never be made to draw a load from home first. if they are to be put in with other cattle, which I like best, let them go from home empty and draw a load toward home first.

George Blanchard, of this town, who has been successful in training steers, has used bits like a horse's, and by this means he has them completely under his command, and can plow between corn and potatoes with either nigh or off ox.

It is quite convenient to have cattle that will back well. This, like everything else, should be learned young. The best way I ever found, was to go directly in front of them and slap each at the same time on the nose, with the open palm of the hand, and both will fly back together. Cattle that are well trained, I am satisfied can back more than they can possibly draw. By hitching their heads next the stone they can lift a larger stone out of a hole than they can draw out, because the chain will draw against the bank the first way. This is convenient in loading stone upon a drag and in laying stone wall. Let me give an illustration. Once two elderly gentlemen, working on the highway, each with a yoke of oxen, made a vain attempt to draw a huge stone out of a hole. They then invited Isaac Damon, my hired hand, to put on my cattle and help them. Damon said, "I will not put my team on with yours, but take yours off and I will get the stone out." They made another trial and gave out, the oldest man saying, "Let the fool try once." While

Damon was hitching the chain into the ring, with the cattle's heads next to the stone, the men standing by eyeing him, he said, "Go along to work, I want you to earn ninepence while I draw out this stone."

These oxen had been so trained to the business, that they would actually hold down their heads for the chain to be fastened. So when he was all ready, with their heads as low as would give them a good footing on the bank, he pronounced an emphatical "back," and out came the stone, much to their astonishment. "There boys," said Damon, "the stone is out." "I would not have believed it," said one of the farmers, "if I had not seen it myself."

I have on a former page recommended bulls in preference to steers, yet large, well trained oxen, to do heavy work on a farm, are decidedly preferable to small ones. There is not so much difference in keeping as is generally supposed. To prove the difference in the work of large and small cattle, I introduce another illustration.

When acting in the capacity of Assessor in this town, I took special notice of the different management of farms, and found the two greatest extremes that came under my eye, lay close together. A youth of fifteen, with a large, handy pair of oxen and good plough, was turning the furrows over straight and clean, on May 1st. Nearby was a man, with a grown son, using a poor plough, with a yoke of cattle and a horse. I noticed that the boy went three rounds to their two, they having frequently to stop and turn the mislaid furrows over with their hands. Here popped into my mind what Franklin said in the eighteenth century.

> The man that by the plough would thrive,
> Himself must either hold or drive.

This man, thought I, was acting up to Franklin's rule, but he was one century behind the times, for we live in a day of great improvements, and the time has already come when

> He that by the plough would thrive
> Will find he must both hold and drive.

Still another illustration. My team of six oxen was driven by my son Horace to plough some hard and rather rocky pasture land, all day, before he was five years of age; and he managed the team as well as a man could have managed it. Here are two considerations,— Horace was a natural teamster, and the team was well trained. I would here add, that an ox that cannot be brought to obedience with fair means, at least without beating and banging, had better be saved the abuse and taken to the slaughter house at once. In short, be kind and gentle to all, yes, all animals.

Was not the farmer and son above referred to, carrying out the theory, "There is no profit in farming," while the youth was as strongly maintaining the position, "There is profit in farming?"

I once knew a man to hire of his neighbor a pair of noble oxen, and a smooth running plough to plough pasture land with some kill-lamb. After using the team and plough a day, he took them home on account of the high price, $1.50 per day. While using this team his son alone ploughed one acre per day, and did the work well. He then hired a smaller pair at 75 cts. per day, and added his horse to make out a team, and went driver himself, the same son holding the plough, and ploughed one-half acre per day, accomplishing in two days more than his son performed in one. Thus it cost the same amount of money for oxen to plough one acre that it cost with the first team, and making an entire loss of two days of his own labor, two days or his horse, and one day of his son's, besides their board. Didn't he try a two-fold experiment, and prove in strong terms both theories before alluded to?

The first stages of education in all animals are highly important. Impressions first given are more enduring and easier made before they come in contact with long established habits.

It is fondly hoped that these few suggestions respecting gentleness and tact in the education of our beasts, will be duly appreciated, pondered and put in practice.

To break a colt to carriage, who is already harness-broken —Put a horse in the carriage that the colt is acquainted with, and ride two or three miles from home. Then change and put the colt in the thills and let another person ride the horse back forward of the carriage and he will be likely to travel homewards after the horse without urging. How many times people harness a colt in their own yard and beat him to drive him away from home against his will, when he knows no more what he is whipped for than a child in the cradle.

All young creatures on their first trial, should have some inducement to urge them on the way you wish them to go. If beaten to make them go against their will, it increases their stubbornness and serves to create a bad disposition. Be careful friends, that you never let your own bad temper serve to create the same bad temper in your animals. How many of the best, noble-spirited horses are ruined through the impatience and indiscretion of their first trainers.

I once bought a horse that had been sold at auction for $15.25. At the time he was sold, he was considered worthless on account of his contrary disposition. He was five years old. I called him "Flying Jib." When I first harnessed him, I treated him very gently, patted his neck and shoulders, breathed in his nostrils, thus making him think he had one friend in the world. I then jumped into the carriage and away he flew. I owned that beast more than one year, and never struck him a blow with a whip or a stick. To pat him with the hand I found much better, and he always started and stopped at bidding, except in one instance, when I was met on the road by a man who had charge of him before I owned him. After speaking a few minutes I told the horse to go, but he refused. I then sat still, the man still continuing talking, and said, "Don't you intend to try to start?"

"Are you willing to go along; if you will, I think my horse will start along too." He then went on muttering in disaffection.

When fairly out of hearing, I said, "Come," and he manifested his usual kindness. Who will say that this horse did not possess a good memory and an inveterate enmity to that man? He never needed a whit of urging to carry me to or from Medford, ten miles, in one hour. This was his natural gait, ten miles per hour. To drive cattle he was the very best. If an ox turned away or stopped to feed, he would turn out after him as quick as a dog, and take hold of the high bunch top of the rump with his teeth. Cattle would soon learn to get out of his way. Although high-spirited, courageous and noble, he was perfectly safe to drive day or night, and if I had him now and knew he was as good as he was when I bought him, I would not take $200 for him.

OMNIBUS STORY—One evening I took a seat in an omnibus at the Cattle Fair Hotel in Cambridge, to ride into Boston. The driver, to admit two ladies, went into the gutter, but the horses refused to take him out. After repeated trials a man came up to tender assistance. The driver became angry and answered tartly. The women were frightened and one insisted on getting out. "If you will keep still," said I, "I will get out and that will lighten the carriage more than two of you, and start the horses if the driver is willing. I accordingly descended, and when the intruder, so considered, had gone away I said to the driver, "May I start your horses and not strike them a blow?"

"Yes, if you can," was the answer.

"Then you shall hold the reins, and when I say 'Come,' run them into the road, but be sure to stop them, and let me get in."

Now that the driver was willing, I had to make the horses willing too. I patted their necks, stroked their faces and breathed in their nostrils. Though utter strangers, I found them the most docile and willing of beasts. Soon each would put his nose on my cheek, our three faces coming in direct contact. I then stepped a little forward, directly in front, looked them in the face, beckoned with both hands and said distinctly, "Come," when they started so quick I was obliged to spring out of the way.

"It took you a great while," said one of the ladies.

"Yes, for I first had to mesmerise the driver, and make him willing."

One of the ladies then asked if I should return that evening.

"I have not fully determined," said I.

"Then I will not go back, if you don't go, although I very much wish to."

"If it would be an accommodation to you to go home, I will return in the 9 o'clock omnibus on these conditions: That you will allow me the pleasure of sitting next to you." This was agreed upon, to the merriment of the company.

We met at the hour appointed, and I never saw her before or since, but one thing I am sure of, she felt safer, as any reasonable woman would, in company with a man who coaxed horses, rather than beat them.

When the driver came for his fare, I offered mine, but he said, "Uncle Asa, I shan't take any pay of you tonight."

"You appear to know me," said I, "but I don't know you."

"Oh, I have known you ever since I was a little boy."

"Then tell me who you are, and perhaps I shall know your father."

When he told his name, "Oh," said I, "I knew your father, and grandfather and great-grandfather, Captain John Harnden, the very man who used to come when I had a broken leg and tell me pleasing stories."

To the young I would say, when you come in contact with old people, if possible make yourself known to them, especially if you have reason to think they have been acquainted with your parents. It is a satisfaction to see the children of their former associates, and if you would introduced yourselves, it would afford them much pleasure. You may sometimes wonder old people do not recognize you, but when you become old yourselves, you can better realize the effect of dim vision and crowded intellect on the mind of the aged.

LICE ON CATTLE

It is vain to expect your stock to thrive while infected with lice. The most simple and effective remedy for them is hog's lard. This should be rubbed or put around the horns, around the ears, between the eyes and nose, the whole length of the back, around the butt of the tail and on the dewlap, and a little in the hollow back of the shoulders, and then let the creature stand in the sun. This should be done once a week, or oftener if you please, as long as a louse can be found. My idea is that they eat so much they split open, for skins can be found two hours after the application. If you have a pen of calves and will let a cosset sheep be put with them and allowed to sleep in the pen, they will have no lice. The lice will leave for warmer lodgings on the sheep and never quit till they have eaten so much of her grease as to kill them. Next to lard I would recommend tobacco wash, which is more trouble and likely to expose the animal to take cold. Never use unguintum on any account. So much for cure. One tablespoonful sulphur in a quart of meal, given once in two weeks, is a sure preventative to lice. It is good for cattle, horses or hogs.

DAIRY WORK

Where a number of cows are kept, it is necessary to set each cow's milk by itself, skim and churn it by itself to ascertain what kind of butter she makes and how long it is in coming. This is important to determine what heifers to keep for milch cows.

I once had fifteen heifers who "came in" so near together that their calves were all taken from them in one day. When they had fairly outgrown their weaning, each one's milk was set separate and the cream churned separate. The result was, one heifer's cream came to butter in about three minutes, eleven of them in ten minutes, and three of them from one and a half to two hours. The first twelve had butter of a nice quality; the last three gave more milk by measure than any of them, but the butter was soft and white. Those I sold to a milkman. Had I kept them with the rest and their cream been churned together, it is my opinion the other heifers' cream would have come to butter, and theirs not at all, but pass off in the buttermilk.

One of my neighbors, famed for good butter and high prices, found one spring that his customers shunned him. On inquiring the cause he was told his butter would not keep well, after three days it could not be eaten. He then tried his cows separately, and found one cow produced butter that smelt badly when first made and when forty-eight hours old could not be endured on the table. He had expected that same cow to be his best dairy cow that season.

One day's cream is a sufficient test, and can be easily stirred to butter in a bowl.

MILKING COWS—Cows should be milked regularly; that is at the same time in the day, every day. This should be done as fast as possible till the last stream is pressed from the udder.

To have all kinds of stock tame, I deem important; more especially milch cows. For this purpose children should be encouraged to feed and play with, and lead them when calves.

BUTTER MAKING—All butter utensils should be kept perfectly sweet and dry, that is, pails, pans, and churns should be dried before being packed away. The milk strainer whether of cloth or wire should be dried as soon as possible. It should be strained in pans about two inches thick as soon as milked and if rich froth remain in the pail a half cup of cold water will settle it, which you may strain into the milk. Twenty-four hours in the hottest weather is long enough to let cream remain on the milk. If it does not keep sweet one day, unless there is thunder, the dishes are not sweet. Cream should always be stirred daily, but in hot weather twice a day, with a stick kept in the creampot, and taken off with as little milk as possible. Forty-eight hours is long enough in any weather for cream to stand on the milk, and thirty six generally. Wind should not blow hard on milk while setting cream, but a draught of air over it greatly facilitates the rising and helps the quality. I should prefer a milk-room with two windows, one north, and one west; this last in hot, sunny days I would shade with an awning to keep out the sun and not obstruct the air. Keep cream covered close, I deem stone pots preferable, and churned twice a week in summer. When taken from the churn, no water should be added but the buttermilk worked out, and salted to liking. After standing till it is cool or till the next morning, it must be again wrought and a half ounce of fine white sugar added to every pound; then weigh and shape for market. The sugar is a preservative and adds to the flavor.

GRAZING—I wish to make a few statements showing the benefits of giving cows good grazing during summer. As I have before said, nothing is so good for making butter as good grass. A few words to illustrate the difference between good and short pasturage. Riding one day with a dairy farmer, I said to him, "A good cow kept in a first rate pasture will be worth $10 more than the same cow kept in a meagre pasture, that is, one had better pay $10 for a good pasture than accept a poor one as a gift."

"Sheldon, I know there is great difference, but I think you are rather wild," said he.

By this time we were passing an excellent pasture on our right, in which two cows were feeding, and a very poor one on the left where three cows were trying to feed.

"Will not those cows make fifty pounds of butter each in a season more than either of the three others?" said I.

"I think they will," said he.

"Will not each cow carry into the barnyard $3 worth more than the others, and won't they on account of their flesh be worth $5 more in the fall?"

"Yes, I think they will," said he, "you have made our your case and more too."

Have we not reason to suppose the owner of the two cows made a profit by farming, while the owner of the three could make no profit?

SHEEP

A few sheep may be profitable to farmers in this section of country if they have a snug pasture, where they will not trouble their neighbors. But back in New Hampshire and Vermont, where butter and milk are less valuable than here, they must be quite profitable. In rearing lambs it should be kept in mind that if a lamb does not get hold of his mother's teat and help himself to what nature has prepared for him, quickly after he is dropped, his life will be short.

When sheep or lambs are poisoned with kill-lamb, so common in New England pastures, a drop or two of warm chamber-lye is certain cure. If the old dam be so unnatural, as sometimes is the case, as to disown her offspring, tie her and take the lamb away and carry it at stated times to suck, holding her the while. Should she still refuse, cuff her ears and she will soon choose to let him suck and have you keep away.

For ticks in sheep, I prefer Jaques' sheep-wash, or extract of tobacco, to anything else. I have tried it on my sheep two different seasons and found that it worked admirable, killing all the vermin, and the sheep thrived afterwards finely.

HOGS

Hogs with proper attention, where manure is valuable, may be made the most profitable of any stock a man can keep on his farm; but if neglected they will run him in debt as fast. The right kind of hogs properly tended, will produce ten pounds pork from one bushel of corn meal, while they may be so neglected and scantily kept that they consume a bushel of meal and not gain a pound. No man can ever get rich by buying a creature and starving it. Hogs are a kind of stock that will not do for a farmer to say he will keep a certain number, let circumstances be as they will.

Whenever it is evident from frost or other reasons that corn will be high, say $2 per barrel, he had better get rid of his hogs, for he never can sell pork high enough to pay the feeding at that price. To make them profitable be sure and keep the best breed, and in a warm pen, with windows to the south, and access to the horse manure for bed, then they will not need bedding every stormy night.

At the time little pigs come, I practice throwing the sow a bit of salt pork; if she eats it readily give her another, and so on till she appears satisfied.

To prevent pigs getting squeezed to death behind the sow, nail a bit of plank, six inches wide, eight inches from the floor of the pen on the side the sow is most likely to lay. This gives room for the pigs to run behind her back and not get squeezed.

HENS

The following article on hens is by Mrs. E. Carter, of Amherst, N. H.

"When living in Wilmington, I thought to get a little pocket money from five hens. I set them on thirteen eggs apiece, and they brought out on an average twelve chickens; many died but what lived were tended regularly, generally fed before the sun was up, oftentimes as soon as out of their coops in the gray of the morning. This fact of an early breakfast, is of great importance to the chicks, as they are faint in the morning and liable to drabble out. I fed them with moist dough twice a day; in the forenoon at twelve o'clock, and in the afternoon at three. I did not scald the meal, but have since found it a great improvement. I kept them on Southern corn-meal at fifty-eight cents per bushel, and sold them off before July ended, leaving a net profit of $11.55 beside the pleasure of tending them. I would strongly recommend a coop for every hen, when her brood is young. They should face the sun, and be built so tall as not to rumple her feathers. This is important. A hen cannot take comfort if anything obstructs her plumage; and for mercy's sake, do not keep them confined day after day, unless in stormy weather. They love liberty, and delight to bask and roll in the sun. Some convenient place should always be provided for them, with ashes to mix with the dirt; it is better for lice than merely dry dirt. If there is nothing of that kind, little ones are apt to die of lice. If the hen and brood are let out the second afternoon of their confinement, they will not be apt to stray far, and return, or be driven to the coop at night, and gladly make that their home. Some boiled potatoes mixed with chicken's dough, I have found many times more profitable than all meal.

I have many times parted the feathers and cut a slit in the crop of a sickly chicken and taken out bad substances, once a hard, black bag, sewed it up again and the chicken would do well, and when picked no trace of stitches could be discovered.

To fatten hens or chickens, they should be shut in a dry pen with a good perch, and fed with new-made corn-meal dough, rather moist, twice per day. After eating the dough, corn should be added, and other grain for change. To add potatoes to the dough for change is beneficial, as they tire of one kind. Some sweeten with molasses, but I never found any profit by it. Nine days is quite long enough to keep them shut up before killing. No water should be used as drink. Where milk is not more than three cents per quart, you will find your account in wetting the dough with new milk every alternate day. The more variations of wholesome food for fattening chickens the better.

In preparing for market, to save tearing the skin, begin to pick as soon as killed, before motion wholly ceases.

It is well known that running fowls lay more eggs in summer than in winter. This I consider owing partly to a lack of meat or meaty substances, which in summer they can help themselves to, in shape of grasshoppers, crickets, bugs, &c. Now, if this lack be supplied by meat orts, from the table or otherwise, and they have a warm house to perch in, and burnt bone or lime constantly by them, with fair water for drink, with some kind of grain, either corn, oats, barley, rye, wheat, or buckwheat, we may expect, when they have rested through the month of December, they will give us very near as many eggs in winter as in summer. In severe cold weather, carry out hot water for them, they will pay back for the delicacy in eggs. A box of ashes to roll in should not be omitted.

I have found it difficult to keep lice out of a hen-house that had been long used for that purpose; but found I could save the chickens by moving the hen and eggs as soon as she wants to set, to some other good place and make a nice nest of straw or meadow hay, either of which are preferable to English hay. Lice will accumulate if she sits in the house, and annoy her so that she often leaves her eggs; should she hatch them they would be likely to die of lice. For this reason coops are recommended as soon as they hatch. We should be as careful to keep our chickens out of the hen pen as to keep our children out of bad company. A shallow, wooden trough is good for the little ones to drink out of in summer.

From my limited experience in different breeds, I have found the Black Spanish the best layers, and Yellow Pennsylvanias the best for market and table purposes.

Some may object to moving a hen lest being disturbed she refuse to set. But if it be done on the first evening, taking her up carefully to avoid rumpling her feathers, and holding her gently on the eggs till she recognizes them, there will be no difficulty in her being satisfied with her new home.

Those who keep their hens shut up on account of the depredations they commit on the garden, or other places, would do well to let them out every afternoon at five o'clock, as they will not then be inclined to scratch on account of their desire to catch insects. To keep them shut up in the forenoon will secure their eggs, as they usually lay before noon.

Since penning the above, I have received from Henry Sheldon, the following safe and tested remedy for lice: One tablespoonful of sulphur to one dozen fowls, mixed with their dough. Repeat the dose on three alternate days. Practice this every two months and your fowls will be healthy, and no lice will trouble them."

CURE FOR HORN AIL, &c.

Make a bag long enough to reach from one horn to the other, and wide enough to reach round the horn, with a string at every corner. Fill it with soft soap and salt mixed, and tie it around the horns. When the bag is in its proper place it will lay partly forward and partly back of the top of the head. You need not stop to ascertain whether the disease be horn-ail or not; if your cattle are dumpish or unhealthy put it on and it will generally bring them to appetite, and surely will do no harm. I have frequently tried it, and always with good effect. I once owned an ox that I kept several years, and some years had to apply it two or three times. I always let it remain until I thought the cure was effected. I have noticed the first symptoms of this disease to be an inclination to hold the head down and a desire to put the nose against something. I cannot say which has the most salutary effect, the medicine penetrating through the skin, or melting and running down to be licked off the nose and thus taken into the stomach. It matters not which makes the cure, but in my opinion both act together. I consider it a very good preventative if applied to a healthy creature.

If you wish your cows to do well at the time of coming in, give them a mess of oats or rye meal every day, awhile beforehand.

Creatures sometimes swell up. I have had oxen that were troubled in this way. One ox that was particularly addicted to it, was so swollen at one time, that a straight stick laying on him would not touch his back. My remedy is: Half a teacup full of ground mustard, half a pint of molasses, half a pint hog's lard and a little water, about milk-warm,— will stir red together,— put in a glass bottle and turn down the throat. Everything given to cattle as a medicine should be milk-warm. Cases of obstructions sometimes occur when injections become necessary to save life. I have had one of this kind used with good success: Take half a pint of lard, two tablespoonsful ground mustard, and as much gunpowder, warm and mix well, and add two quarts warm water.

If the udder of a cow be swollen or inflamed at time of coming in, put a tablespoonful of saleratus in a quart of warm water, and bathe it therewith. It works to a charm.

For scratches in horses, bathe in blubber oil every alternate day, till a cure is effected.

PLOUGHS AND PLOUGHING

In my humble opinion there has been no radical improvement in ploughs for the last thirty years. Far be it from me to discourage improvements, but although I see alterations they do not appear to be beneficial. Between the year 1800 and 1830, there were great improvements in ploughs. The best plough that I ever used was built by Deacon Benjamin Foster, of this town, in the year 1816. This plough was a perfect machine in every respect. If it laid on the wing when you started the team, the first motion would cause it to come up square on its bottom. In common grass ground it would turn a furrow sixteen inches wide and lay it over so neatly that if a man could see neither center nor outside, it would trouble him to tell which way the furrows were turned. Where there were neither roots nor stones, it would run the whole length of the furrow without holding. Put it into an old corn field, and walk beside your team, and it would run from side to side, splitting the hills without your touching it, as well as any plough could possibly do it by being guided. Out of $300 worth of ploughs that I have owned since, this was the only one that I ever found that would do it. I do not know the weight of this plough, but wish I did. Of one thing I am certain, it was not more than half as heavy as the ploughs we now use, that will turn a furrow of the same width.

The next best plough I ever owned was made by Warren, of North Danvers. This had a rolling cutter and run easily for the team, being a light plough in proportion to the furrow it cut. The great error plough makers have fallen into within the last thirty years, is by increasing the weight so much it over balances every other improvement. It is worth one mill for a team to carry one pound a day. Now if a plough be fifty pounds heavier than need be, there is five cents loss every day in carrying that weight, besides the ploughman's extra labor in throwing it round at ever corner, and have thought ever since my leg was broken, that was worth ten cents extra. If plough builders would give us any improvement in ploughs, I beg them to make them lighter.

Cutters to all ploughs should be so made as to cut a little under on the land side. By that means the furrows can be dropped in flat. I would not have a man plow grass land and lap the furrows, if he would do it for nothing. The disadvantage of tilling that year would more than overbalance the cost of plowing.

Depth of plowing should vary according to circumstances. Land should never be plowed very deep the first time. Land five inches below the surface on virgin soil is softer and lighter than ever afterwards. I learned this when a boy, by observing when breaking new land the oxen's feet who trod in the furrow would settle in deeper than in an old field.

If you have but little manure be sure and not plow too deep, from five to seven inches; but if manure is abundant you may plow from eight to nine inches with profit.

SWALE LAND

There is a kind of swale land generally covered with alders, which is excellent for grass if rightly managed. Frequently on examination, white sand may be found within two inches of the surface. If so, never plough it. Cut the alders close to the ground and burn them in the month of August; sow on grass seed; spread on plenty of compost manure, a great part of which may be dirt; use a brush-harrow unsparingly, and next July you may expect a noble crop of herd's grass and red-top, taking it for granted you sowed that kind of seed. In haying time there will most probably be some alder sprouts that the scythe will readily take off, and the stock the next winter will not object to them at all,

and likely they will be the last that will spring up. This
land will ask for a little grass-seed about every five years,
and top dressing at the same time. I have no doubt one-half
the manure made from this grass will, by composting, keep
the land highly dressed, giving you the privilege of selling
one-half the crop. I have no doubt but that in this way your
land will yield a good crop more years in succession than I
have lived. This is the most profitable way of raising
English grass I have ever found.

RECLAIMING SWAMP LAND

The first object is to drain it. Dig a central ditch, and one on
each side. At the downstream end, dig a ditch from the side
ones into the central one. After the draining, the main surface will settle, the old harrock grass will die, and in about
one year it will be in a fit condition to clear the wood and
bushes away, which should be done by cutting the roots as
they become prominent. It is not profitable to do this till
one year after drainage. Don't be too particular about getting all the old settlers out, but plant with potatoes without
manure; they will thrive well among the roots in close
proximity to a stump, which time will loosen with each
revolving year. Avoid cross ditches, they are troublesome in
plowing. If the swamp land is good it will bear better
potatoes two years without than with manure. The farmer
can judge when the land wants manure, by the length of
the potato vines. If they are six or seven feet long, there is
no need of manure; if only four feet, put some manure in
the hill.

In tilling this virgin soil, it will be discovered that the
surface is the best. My manner of planting is to deposit the
seed on the top and hoe dirt upon them. As I continue to
till, I go deeper in order to bring up new soil. I sometimes
plant several years before I plough a furrow. I cannot say

how long it will hold out, but I have a piece which I planted eight years that yields a satisfactory crop.

This kind of land will bear good herd's grass, &c., four years, after that wild grasses come in plentifully. Potatoes grow here of good quality, but grass, although very handsome, has not the sweetness of upland hay. It ought then to be ploughed, and grass seed sown again, or potatoes planted, and at every ploughing I would attempt to strike a little deeper than before.

Mud from ditches, such as mentioned above, is superb to spread on the land among young apple trees in the fall, and plow in, in the spring.

RAISING CORN, POTATOES AND GRASS

These three articles are classed together because the good farmer's object is, while he raises the two first to produce the third. Let us suppose an acre of ground, well adapted to all these, but has been in grass so long that it produces only from ten to fifteen hundred weight to the acre. I would plough the land in August, if the soil be suitable, eight or nine inches deep. If you intend to lay it down after the first crop of corn is taken off, put on all the manure it will need for seven years, and spread on the ground. Then run a light plow lengthwise of the furrows, as deep as you can and not disturb the sod. This work should be finished in September, and the land rest through the winter. In the spring you may harrow, or cross-plough as you choose; then mark the land in rows both ways three and a half feet apart for corn-planting — four kernels to the hill is sufficient. Corn should always be hoed three times and more rather than let it get weedy. The weeds should be kept down at any rate, and if this is done the plough or cultivator will do most of the work; the hoeing labor is but light. I can testify from experience that no man can make a profit by raising weeds.

Be sure and plant early corn, and if you are going to sow down, cut up the corn, stalks and all, as soon as it is fairly out of the milk. Shock it in the field, taking up as little ground as you can. Then plow, but without disturbing the old sods; they have a duty to do to the coming grass crop, where they are. When ready sow one peck of herd's grass and one bushel red-top to the acre. You will be under the necessity of leaving narrow strips where the shocks are, but these you must prepare and sow as soon as you can.

Now if you have put fifteen cords of manure to the acre and followed these directions, you may expect from seventy to one hundred bushels of corn to the acre, and a noble lot of corn-fodder; and an average of two tons of hay to the acre for the first four years; one and a half tons for the next two years, and if not convenient to plough again then, you need not be afraid of its being poorer than when first ploughed for three years more.

ANOTHER WAY OF RAISING CORN AND POTATOES—Let the cornhills remain till spring. Drop potatoes on to the ground directly between the hills, then throw manure on to them; take a pair of oxen or a horse and split the hills, two furrows in a row, throwing the dirt on to the potatoes. A man should walk over the ground and re-cover if necessary, or hoe off if a surplus remains. A few days before they show themselves above ground, drag a brush harrow crosswise over the ground; this will disturb the weeds and give the potatoes a chance to get ahead of these dwellers on the sod. When ready to hoe, plough crosswise the furrows and then follow the with hoe. Twice tending is all that is generally needed, for it is always injurious to work among them after the vines spread. In this way you will be able to get from two to three hundred bushels to the acre. This mode I learned from a man in Connecticut, when I was teaming hops to New York. It may be thought by some a slovenly way, but my word for it, it is the cheapest, easiest and most profitable way that I ever knew potatoes raised on upland.

After the crop is taken off, the land will be ready to sow with grass.

A DAY'S WORK — When I arose in the morning the manure was in the barnyard, the potatoes lay in the barn uncut, and the ground lay in Indian hills just as the corn was taken from it the fall before. I commenced operations with Daniel Eames, who loaded and teamed out all the manure, laying it in heaps; while I with three small children, (the youngest not five years old), dropped the potatoes, laid on the manure, and covered by splitting the hills. From that day's work I realized over five hundred bushels of potatoes. I have ever been in favor of this mode of raising potatoes, no matter how hard the ground is under them.

Two farmers, well known to me, and to each other, planted each a patch of corn on land much infested by witchgrass. One plowed his ground just before planting, then gathered up what grass was handy into bunches and burned it. As soon as the corn was out of the ground and would possibly admit of hoeing, it was ploughed and hoed. And this process was continued every week for seven successive weeks. I have heard the owner say that when hoeing it passersby would say, "what are you hoeing that corn for, it don't need it?" His answer was, "I don't mean it shall this summer." In consequence of stirring the ground so often and keeping the grass in subjection the crop came forward and matured early, and was a most beautiful crop of sound corn.

The other man cleared off the witch grass after ploughing as did the former, and treated it in other respects equal till the corn was planted. The first hoeing was put off till the grass covered all the surface as high as the corn, and hoed but twice in the season. He observed to me that he thought it cost him as much labor to hoe his twice as it did his neighbor to hoe his seven times, but not so much to plough it. In September it was thought that this field was about two weeks behind the other, and an early frost coming, there was not much sound corn; mostly hog-corn.

If you want a good crop of corn, stir the ground often till the weeds have done coming up. A moment's reflection will show the difference in tending an acre where the weeds are ten inches high, and where they are just peeping from the ground. In some sections tending only twice is practiced; and those who practice it generally hoe late, after the weeds are grown, and with as much labor as would tend the same ground three times in the proper season, and secure a better crop. In this case the old maxim is verified: "A stitch in time saves nine."

RAISING ROOTS

Old pasture land is preferable for nearly all kinds of roots. It should be ploughed the previous August, and will not be so subject to weeds or worms as old fields. Many times half the labor is thus saved.

For rutabagas no matter how sandy the land is. The best crop I ever raised was on blowing sand. I furrowed quite deep and applied the rawest manure from the barn cellar. After it was placed in the bottom of the furrows, a light sprinkling of sand was hauled over it; I then sowed the seed with a machine, about the last of June, and realized the best crop of bagas I ever raised or ever saw. I had eighty-two barrels on one-fourth of an acre. Sold them to one man for sixty-seven cents per barrel. Rutabagas depend almost entirely on the manure. As to soil, there was none there, but the heavens gave water that kept them well sprinkled and the manure well soaked.

Parsnips and carrots require a good loamy soil, with old rotten manure well sprinkled and the manure well mixed with the soil. I think they grow larger and longer on ridges, than on level surface.

FOREST TREES

To make an oak growth profitable, it should be cut once in twenty-five years. If the owner be paying interest money and wood turns well, he had better not let it stand over twenty-two years. For the benefit of the sprouts that come after, it should be cut some time when the days are shorter than the nights. The stumps should be cut very close to the ground for several reasons:

1st. Because you get more wood.

2d. It is much better getting over the land with sled or wagon.

Last, but not least by any means, sprouts coming from a stump near the ground, thrive much better than those starting from a stump six inches above the ground.

If you cannot bend your own back, nor persuade your chopper to do so, you had better cut your trees in early fall so that the stump may dry by the sun and die on the top, and the sprouts start out near the ground.

I once sold a lot of standing oak wood at auction. Aged men that were there said it was so thrifty that it was a sin to cut it. It amounted to $75 per acre. The whole growth was taken away before the first day of April. No cattle were allowed on it for four years. I would rather a man would drive hungry cattle through my mow-land, than to drive the same number through my sprout-land.

Twenty-two years from the time of the auction, in looking over the lot, I made up my mind that it would fetch $50 per acre, if put up at auction. It was sold at $65 per acre. This was three and a half years ago, and there is now as fine a growth of sprouts on it as I ever saw on any land.

Reckoning $75 for twenty-five and a half years, at six per cent., compound interest, amounts to $340.45; and $65 for three and a half years, at the same rate, amounts of $79.25; making a total of $419.70 per acre. Drawing conclusions from a lot that stood near by, and larger than mine at the time of the first auction, mine would at this time be worth not more than $125 per acre had the first growth stood. I would particularly say here, that sprouts coming from a young growth are worth more in twenty years than those coming from an old growth are in forty.

A lot of wood is now standing within my knowledge, that I recollect a man offered $200 per acre for the top in 1812. I have often passed that lot and never noticed a tree cut from it from that day to this. Had this offer been taken and the money put at compound interest at this time, it would amount to the amazing sum of $3817 per acre, and another growth would have sprung up fifty years old, probably worth $83 per acre, swelling the sum to $3,900 per acre.

Last week I looked over the same lot, and cannot call it worth more than $300 per acre, showing a dead loss of $3,600 per acre. I have been told that there are ten acres in the lot, and if so there is $36,000 loss to the owner by not turning his property.

Young men, don't be alarmed at this statement; figures do not lie.

When cutting off an oak lot, if you wish to clear the land for pasturing, let the brush lay on the ground until July, then burn it as it lays. If any sprouts or bushes remain after the fire, cut them all; rake everything into piles and burn them. Sow one bushel of rye to the acre, one peck of herd's grass seed, one bushel red top, and a few pounds of white clover. Harrow in well, and be sure that this operation is performed by the first of August. Winter rye should be on the ground nearly one year, I know from experience, and the grass will do much better. By this method you may expect a good crop of grain, and the straw is no small item, selling for about three-fourths the price of English hay, which has been the case for several years.

If the land is strong, you will probably choose to mow two or three years before pasturing it. This I like, because the scythe will cut off the young sprouts at the very time they ought to be cut.

Whenever a pine lot is cut off, and another growth is desired, be sure to have some of the largest trees on the highest ground to seed the land. A pine growth will follow a pine growth quicker if you burn the boughs and sow rye first, without grass.

The seed of the pitch-pine matures the first year; white-pine seed does not till the second — this I am certain of, and if a man should tell me that it did not till the third, I would not dispute him. An abundance of them start but few come to maturity.

To save pine seed, pick the cones from the tree immediately after the first hard frost, put them in a cask and set them under cover. The seed is about as big as an apple seed, each having two wings. And if the cone remain on the tree, as fast as they open the wind will waft them away.

A growth of pitch-pine should be cut off between twenty-five and thirty years. White-pine will make beautiful timber in about fifty years. The value of white-pine timber is increased by cutting at the last of August or the first of September, and peeling the bark off. Then no worm will ever touch it. If I were building a house, I would not take the gift of timber cut in June; it will powder post, depend upon it.

It sometimes occurs that land, where you would like to have pines come in, is swarded over with grass so as to prevent the seed from germinating. This can be remedied by going over it with a plough, and turning it a little to the left a narrow strip may be cut out that will answer all purposes.

A man owning several acres of pine woodland, in anticipation of cutting off a piece at a time would do well to run a plough wherever he expects to need a partition fence, and the seed will come in rapidly. Should nature leave gaps in her sowing, the defect may be easily remedied by small pines.

A reliable friend who owned several hundred acres pine land assured me he had seven miles of this fence, what he called "living pine." He said it cost him but little pains and care, and he would not exchange it for the best rail fence, or pine plain, that could be found.

KING TREE—At one time I bought a quantity of standing wood on Tay's East Mountain,—the top of which is crowned with a basin of water, never dry,—of Loammi Baldwin, Esq., with a specified time to clear it off. At the time of cutting and clearing he was absent in one of the Carolinas, engineering a dry dock. Knowing the Baldwins to be men of curious mind, very fond of landmarks, I thought, while lying in bed, that if Mr. Baldwin were at home he would redeem a prominent white-pine tree which stood on the brow of the hill. I came to the conclusion that the tree should not be cut till he returned. The first time I saw him, he said, "Sheldon, I have been past the mountain lot and noticed one tree standing there; why didn't you take that away? In every other particular you have cleared the lot according to agreement." I told him the fact, that in my night-musings I had thought he might value that tree standing, more than its real worth in dollars and cents.

"How much is that tree worth?" said he.

"Five dollars," I replied.

Whereupon he took from his pocket $25 and gave it to me, saying "That is to pay you for thinking for me when I don't think for myself. Last winter, when at the South, I awoke one night and thought of that King tree. I wished that I had reserved it, and would gladly have given twice its value, but never expected to see it again. Now I would not take a hundred dollars for it, not that it will be worth that in cash, but because it will afford me pleasure in riding over the neighboring towns, to see that landmark and recall the pleasant thoughts associated with it."

No man can calculate the cords of wood that will grow

from the seed of that tree, standing as it does on an elevation where the wind fans it from all directions.

I would here intimate to the young, never to be in haste to fell a tree that you have reason to believe another person would take comfort in having stand. When once down it cannot be replaced again. I have known lasting animosities created between families and friends by the simple but significant fact of cutting a favorite tree. Sure I am there is not a prominent tree in the country but that some one would not like to see it fall.

On the day that I was seventy years of age, I set an elm tree, and the day that I was seventy-one I set fifteen, all of which are alive and doing well. I make it a rule, not to be broken, to set one or more trees on every birthday, which occurs at the very best season to transplant trees.

Walnut trees are the most difficult to transplant and make live, by reason of the taproot running down like a parsnip. If you can select one growing on a ledge where there is no length of taproot, it can be transplanted without trouble, but be sure and place the same side to the South that stood there in its natural state.

White-pine trees can be safely transplanted the first days in June. My friend, Deacon Levi Parker, assured me that he set one hundred some years since, and only three died; ninety-seven are thriving.

APPLE TREES

Nurseries should be planted on high land, free from stone. In the fall is the best time for planting them. I like to have the rows so far apart as to have a row of roots grow between them. The land should not be very highly manured; if it is, the trees will not acquire as many roots as they need after transplanting. If they grow on land free from stone they can be taken up much easier, and without bruising the roots so badly. As soon as the trees are big enough, bud them in the month of August. After one year's growth from the bud, the old stock should be cut off in the following spring. Two years after budding, either fall or spring, is the right time to transplant the tree. Three years will answer, but I had rather have it one year than four.

Before you take up the tree, tie a string to a limb that projects toward the South, and be sure you set it in the same direction in transplanting. Many a tree has been nearly ruined by having its North side exposed to the hot rays of the sun in July. I had rather have five trees set as they grew in the nursery, than six turned round.

If you set an orchard, be sure that your land is suitable for it. Hilly land with loamy surface and clayish gravel sub-soil is best. Land where walnut grows is sure to favor apple trees, and you need not be at all afraid to set them where barberries grow.

In early pruning, be sure to leave branches where you want them; if one is nothing but a bud it will be a branch if the others are cut away. When I first commenced rearing an orchard, I was advised to leave three branches only to form the tree. Experience has taught me that five is much better, for with only three branches the wind has often an opportunity to strike sidewise of a branch, sometimes to the injury of the tree.

A forked tree you had better cut off and graft anew or throw away, as it is not worth raising. The wind will split it and cause you to lose your labor.

I am not fond of setting trees so far apart as many far-mers are. Thirty feet is quite enough. I would rather have them only twenty-five than to have them thirty-five. Wind has more power where trees are set a long distance apart, than where nearer together. The limbs of trees in an or-chard will generally meet even where the trees are set forty feet apart; and a bushel of apples on a limb twenty feet from the trunk of the tree will strain it more than the same number would at fifteen feet. When the orchard is first set, it is a good thing to mulch them with straw or poor meadow hay, laying on some stones to keep it from blowing away. This is quite indispensable if the season be dry.

TRIMMING TREES — The very best time to trim a tree is the day the blossoms begin to open. But this lasts only a few days, and in a busy season, and if put off until it is a little too late will prove an injury, therefore I cannot recommend it. The best time that I can recommend is near the time when the sun crosses the line, either in March or September. Sometimes the Spring is so very forward there is danger of trimming in the last days of March. In proof of this let me say, that I have one orchard which I have allowed to be trimmed in the month of March only, and must say I know of no healthier trees in the County of Middlesex. In cutting off the limb, you should be careful not to cut the seam that joins the limb to the tree, as this course will make a larger wound and will require a longer time to heal.

I would advise every young farmer to select a tree and cut off a limb every month in the year, and thus he will find out by experiment how the sap works and which time is best. This should be noted in a book to avoid mistake.

Young trees should be washed with a corn broom, with strong soap suds and ashes, to prevent the first start of moss, as soon as the frost is out of the ground in the Spring, and again in October. This will prevent lice and help to keep out borers. They should be carefully looked over before the leaves start, to take off every caterpillar's egg.

After an orchard is set, I like to plant corn. Care should be taken to row both ways, and every tree take the place of a hill that they may not obstruct ploughing. In a few years I like to plant squashes between them. Should you choose to lay down to grass, do not let it remain so more than three years lest the trees become stunted.

Black swamp mud, spread on an orchard in the Fall and ploughed in and mixed with the soil in the spring, is excellent for the trees.

In gathering apples, place the thumb against the stem so as to break it at the first joint. A good faithful boy is better to pick apples than a man. The lighter he is the better, if he understands his business. Shoes or boots with nails in the heels, should not be used. Apples should be gathered before the ground freezes at night; packed in a cask; set in a cool place, and kept from air as much as possible.

The most profitable apple to raise in large quantities, is the Baldwin. They are a sure bearer once in two years, and always sell for ready cash at market price. They ripen so that all can be gathered at once, and as soon as they are ready for market, the market is generally ready for them; and the farmer will receive more net profit from a Baldwin tree than from any other, compared with the expense.

The origin of the Baldwin apple has been much disputed. Many are willing to claim it, but from authentic sources, I have gained the information that it was a wild tree taken from the woods in the South part of Wilmington, on what is called Wood-hill, by William Butters, and transplanted and set about fourteen rods from his back door. From that tree Colonel Loammi Baldwin cut scions for his own orchard, from which originated the name. On that point there was so much dispute, I felt an interest in knowing, if possible, where it was first produced. The first evidence was gained from James Butters, who lived on Wood-hill. He informed me that the tree was taken from land of his, and frequently urged me to go and see the hole where it was taken out of; and the last time I well remember his words, "You will be sorry if you don't." His words proved true.

I once heard that the tree was claimed in North Tewksbury, and made a journey up there to see what proof could be afforded of it. I was showed a tree they called a Baldwin, but it bore little resemblance to the Baldwin trees of Wilmington. I know of no better way to describe it, than by calling it a two-story tree. I did not see any of the fruit, nor could I find a man in the neighborhood that was able to give any information as to where the tree came from. Simeon Butters, son of James before mentioned, showed me, as near as he could recollect, where the tree stood when it bore fruit; and at another time Walter Butters showed me the same, and they did not vary four feet. Likewise the widow of Loammi Baldwin identified the same spot. I asked all three of the last mentioned persons what became of that tree. The first said, "The tree was thrifty when I went to live in Lynn eight years ago, but when I came back I never noticed it afterward." The second could tell nothing about it. I then repaired to the woman and asked her, "Can you tell me what became of that tree?" "I guess I can," she replied. "The day that I was married there came up a shower just before twelve o'clock, and lightning tore that tree all to pieces."

The Red Astrican grows very handsome and thrifty; the apple is first ripe about the tenth of August, and is continually ripening for five weeks. They require picking as often as once in two days. This apple is not suitable for eating but for about four days, consequently it must be carried to market often. At the present time they bring a good price on account of the scarcity.

The Gravenstein is an excellent apple for eating; everybody likes the flavor of it. It is scarce in market and commands a high price.

The Hubbardston-Nonesuch is a very good apple; some prefer it to the Baldwin, but it will not keep as long.

The Blue Pearmain grows large, but is not a good winter apple, and is not so profitable to raise as the Baldwin.

The Maiden's Blush is a great bearer and grows fair. It is a first rate pie apple.

The Early Sweetbow grows fair and large, and is a first rate eating apple.

The Orange Sweet grows in clusters of four and six, touching each other. The tree is rather small in size, with upright branches, and bears largely. They ripen the last of August.

The Striped Sweet is first rate for eating or baking, and sell high.

The Green Winter-Sweet is an excellent bearer; very fair; small core; good for use all winter; keep till June, and the worms never trouble them.

Wine apple; tree handsome; thrifty grower; upright branches; fruit small in size, but fair and red from skin to core.

Iron apple; small in size; very hard; never fit to eat raw; good for pies and sauce when one year old, and will keep till September.

The best time to cut scions is the day you want to set them. But this is not always convenient; in that case they should be buried in a box of loam. The first new moon in May is the best time for grafting. If you hire grafting done, be sure to employ an honest man. I once employed men who set by the scion, and when I was absent they were seen to cut scions from the same tree and set them. When the trees bore fruit, the truth was told.

CRANBERRIES

Incidental experience has shown me that cranberries can be cultivated to good advantage. In several places where sandhills have been removed for the purpose of making embankments on railroads, the sand was taken down as low as could be for water, and afterwards freshets had washed cranberries on from the meadows above. In three years they begun to bear, and I know that, one year, the crop was worth $100 per acre on the vines. If one wishes to cultivate cranberries, the surest way would be to select a spot on a brook that never fails, and have it graded as level as a salt marsh. Then make a dam above and one below to let on water and take it off at pleasure. This process will sometimes be needed in a cold night in June, and a dry time in July or August to soak the ground and give growth to the berry and destroy worms, and in cold nights in September to keep off frost, that they may ripen on the vines. In these circumstances, I think a man may be as sure of a crop of cranberries as of a crop of corn. A brook privilege being secured, the best location is where a sandy plain joins a meadow, and in lowering one you raise the other. Sand is the best manure for Cranberries. The vines should becovered with two feet of water through the winter season to prevent the ice from adhering to the ground and taking it up.

❖❖❖

CONCLUSION

Before I bring this volume to a close let me say a word or two upon a subject which has for many years engaged my attention. I do not intend to bore my readers with anything lengthy; I merely wish to give them my opinions upon a subject which interests us all. The motives which lead me to do this, need not necessarily be given, therefore I will proceed.

The doctrine of "total depravity" has been preached and expatiated upon for generations and generations, when it had nothing, to my mind, for a foundation. I cannot so far forget my obligations to God as to suppose for a moment that he is the author of a totally depraved being. Men may sin, and to human eyes appear totally depraved, but to the all-seeing eye of God I cannot think they so appear. I believe God to be the creator and father of all mankind; I believe him to be holy, just, wise and pure, perfect in everything; I believe he created man after his own image and in his own likeness; but I cannot believe that God has created a world full of children without one particle of goodness in any of them. If you were digging for gold and had taken a handful of earth, expecting by washing it to find gold, but which did not contain any, you might wash it all away and you would find no gold. Now if man is totally depraved there can be nothing in him worth saving. This I do not, I cannot, I will not believe. We are God's rebellious children, yet he knows how to separate the gold from the dross. What proportion of us will come forth as gold, God only knows. Do right and trust the event. Forget not that Christ said, "By their works ye shall know them." In the Bible we read, "And the books were opened; and another book was opened, which is the book of life; and the dead were judged out of those things that were written in the books, according to their works." Here, certainly, we find great encouragement to live a good, moral life. How shall we do this? My friends, young and old, if you have not already done it, adopt the rule today, to do unto others as you would have them do unto you. Follow this rule, and you will soon love God, and he will be sure to love you. It may not make you rich, but my word for it, it will make you happy. Some may say, that there are none that do as they would be done by, but this I will not admit. I have been acquainted with mankind more than seventy years, and have come to this conclusion, that the best of men do in their daily walk live near to God, and that there are grades all the way down until the worst come so near the devil that it is hard to discriminate between them. I have been, for a certain reason, watching the conduct of men for more than thirty years in order to find as many as I could that lived up to this rule, and I feel it my duty to set before my readers the names of some of them, that others may be encouraged to do likewise.

Accordingly I publish a list of the names of men who I defy mankind to prove by truth-telling witnesses, before a righteous jury, that they ever used another man worse than they would be willing to be used in exchange of conditions: Ephraim Hastings, died at Nashua, N. H.; Lambert Hastings, St. Johnsbury, Vt.; Cyrus Skinner, Lyme, N. H.; Dexter Fay, Southborough, Amos Hill, Jr., Belmont, John Buckman, Stoneham, Charles Goddard, Winchester, Isaac Flint, North Reading, Ebenezer D. Batchelder, North Reading, Jonathan Batchelder, North Reading, Marshall Symmes, Winchester, Charles S. Storrow, Lawrence, Eben King, Eben Upton, South Danvers, Edward Parker, Reading, Capt. David Graves, North Reading, Patrick T. Jackson, Boston, Deacon Henry Putnam, Joseph Batchelder, John Batchelder, of North Reading, Col. Benjamin Jenkins, Samuel Jenkins, Capt. Stephen Abbott, of Andover, Deacon John Symmes, Winchester. The thirteen last named persons are dead. All these men I have known for many years, and think there are thousands of other good men of my acquaintance whom I have not proved through prosperity and adversity. Those that I have named I have proved, and can bear testimony that they are not depraved men. What a blessed world this would be to live in, if every one would do as he would be done by. Now reader, do not fall into the error of believing that you cannot do right because others do not. If a right state of feeling is ever brought about, it will be by each and every one minding his own business. I hope that you and I shall try it, that others may follow.

LECTURE

In the month of February, 1859, I was invited by the officers of the Farmer's Club, of North Reading, to address them on the subject of Farming. I accepted, and delivered the following address, with which I close this volume, before the Club, in the Town Hall, at that place.

MR. PRESIDENT, GENTLEMEN AND LADIES — I have no apology to offer, for appearing before you this evening. I will only say, that any common man ought to feel proud of the privilege of standing before the combined wisdom and intelligence of the Farmers of North Reading, and addressing them on a subject of more importance to the world than all others.

When I say farmers, I mean fathers, mothers, sons and daughters; for as no house can stand when divided against itself, so no man can farm successfully if his family are not content with that occupation. The few remarks that I shall make this evening, are not to tell you how to farm, but —

1st. To prove to you that farming, with equal system, is the most profitable occupation pursued within the United States.
2d. It is the most independent.
3d. It is the most healthy.
4th. It is the most honorable.

First. Farming, with equal system, is the most profitable occupation within the United States. This you may think, is a bold declaration, but if you will have patience, I will give you the proofs.

If the country merchant fails in his business, he generally owes some of the most fore-handed farmers in his neighborhood, money that he borrowed to establish him in his business. If the butcher fails, he owes one farmer for a pair of fat oxen, another for a cow, and still another for a hog. So, if the tanner fails, he is indebted to one farmer for a load of bark, another for hides, and a third for calfskins. If the carpenter fails, he is indebted to one farmer for timber and a second for boards. If the shoe manufacturer fails, he owes one farmer for a load of wood, another for a load of hay, and almost every farmer's daughter in the parish for binding shoes. Yet with all these losses, the farmer still lives; and why? Because there is profit in his occupation.

Now, gentlemen, show me a man sixty years of age, of good health, good habits, and good common sense, who has never followed any business but that of farming, and I will show you a man that the world has never lost one cent by.

Mr. President, I have already stated that unless the farmer has the hearty co-operation of his family he cannot succeed in his business. These ladies may inquire how can we increase the profits of farming. To this inquiry, I would answer, Ethan Allen understood how you could do this. When taken a prisoner to England, the nobility there, finding that he was a man of good sense and information, had him taken into the presence of the ladies that they might question him concerning the habits of the Americans. Among the many questions asked him was this: "What time do the ladies of America walk out for pleasure?" His answer was, "Any time when the hens, turkeys, geese or ducks need feeding." "Do the ladies of America stoop to feeding poultry?" they inquired. He answered, "The ladies of America know how to turn every duty into a pleasure." This *was* the case with the ladies at the time of the Revolution, and I know from my own observation that there are some of the same stamp yet.

A few years ago I noticed in the papers an advertisement of a large farm, with a heavy growth of wood and timber on it, for sale in New Hampshire. Thinking that it might be bought at a bargain, I went to look at it. A young lady answered my knock at the door, and informed me that her father was absent with the team and would not return until evening, "but," said she, "if you will state your business, perhaps I can assist you." On learning that I wished to go over the farm, telling me to wait one moment, she went into the house, but soon returned, dressed in hat, frock, and boots, and we started on our walk. After pointing out three of the boundaries of the farm, she told me where I could easily find the fourth, "but," said she, "I must now go, and tie up the cattle." After walking about the farm as long as I wished, I met her at the barn. She had just finished tying up the cattle, and invited me to look at the corn. This I did, and my guide informed me that it had all been measured in the ear, and estimated to be four hundred bushels shelled corn, and that she and her father planted it all, she dropping and her father covering. From the corn barn we proceeded to the house, where it was arranged that I should stop over night to see the owner of the farm. Our heroine now laid aside her farm dress, appearing as neatly dressed as any young lady could wish to be, and assisted her mother in preparing supper. As soon as the team was heard approaching, she again put on her frock, and lighting a lantern, went to the barn and helped her father put up the team. This done, we all ate supper. After clearing away the tea-things, my young friend again prepared to go out, and in answer to her father's inquiry where she was going, replied, "to feed the oxen." "No, no," said he, "I'll go." "No, father," she instantly replied, "you are tired, you sit still and rest, and let me go," and go she did, after which she seated herself at her piano and entertained us for a while with music.

Mr. President, if I could mention a thousand young women like this instead of one, which I sincerely wish I could, I presume we should not hear of one of them being troubled with dyspepsia.

But there is still another profit in farming, that cannot be estimated by dollars and cents. It is better calculated to improve the mind and morals of man than any other occupation. The reflecting farmer must see that he is a co-worker with God and Nature. While he is cultivating his crops, and they are growing in the fields, he cannot help observing this. When the grass is grown, and man cuts it, nature cures it, and God sustains them both.

Second. Farming is the most independent occupation. No other occupation can live without it. No ship can be laden without the aid of the farmer. No cultivated food can be raised for man or beast, without his labor. Why, ladies, the very silks you wear were once the habitation of worms, those worms fed on mulberry leaves, and the mulberry trees raised by the farmer. Not one particle of food or raiment can be produced without his aid.

It has been said by many that the Irish have performed the labor of building our railroads. But, Mr. President, allow me to tell you that more than one-half the money the Irish have received for labor on railroads has been spent for their living, while doing that very work, and this living, was produced by the farmer. This shows us that the farmer has not been backward in doing his share toward building all the railroads in the United States. And who is it, I ask, that now furnishes these railroads with employment? Who produces the horses, cattle, sheep, hogs, wheat, rye, barley, oats, potatoes, apples, cotton, wool, and almost every article that can be mentioned, that are daily transported on our railroads? It is the farmer. If the farmer should cease to produce cotton, wool, flax and hemp, what would become of our factories?

If a new country is to be settled, who is the pioneer? Is it the minister? No, for he would starve while studying his first sermon. Is it the doctor? No, for there is no one there with whom he could exchange his medicine for a dinner. Is it the lawyer? No, for he would perish amid his law books. Who, then, is it? It is the farmer, who feeds all, and gives employment to all. Farmers have it in their own power to render themselves happier and more independent than they now are. In order to do this, they must raise their standard to its proper place. The farmers of Massachusetts can outvote all other occupations by a large majority. They possess the power to elect any man, from any occupation, to any office they please. I would not ask them to be domineering over any other class of people. I am willing that all other classes shall have their full share of representation in every department of government. But have the farmers, in times past, looked out to have *their* share? Have we not sent to General Court and to Congress, too many professional men? Has not this led ministers, doctors and lawyers to look down upon the farmer, when in reality, if the farmer would but assert his rights, they would all be obliged to look up to him.

I could say much more, under this head, but enough has already been said, I think, to prove that the farmer furnishes all other classes with food and employment. Mr. President, when I think of the farmer's position, and compare it with all others, it reminds me of a story I heard when a boy.

Three men, travelling together in a wild country, became very thirsty, but travelled a long time without finding any water. At length, however, they came to a river, the banks of which were composed of a perpendicular ledge of stone. Not seeing any way of descent, they travelled on until they discovered a tree growing from a seam in the ledge, whose branches extended over the water, but were several feet above it. After a hasty consultation, they came to this conclusion. The stoutest man of the three was to climb the tree, and taking hold of a branch, hang down; the next stoutest to hang by the feet of the first, while the third, the lightest of the whole, was to hang by the feet of the second, and fill a leather bag with water from the stream, and bring it up for them to drink. While he was filling the bag, the upper one, growing tired, says to his comrades, "you hold fast, while I let go and spit on my hands."

Now, Mr. President, this shows what would be the condition of all occupations, if the farmer should cease his operations. All would sink together.

Third. Farming is the most healthy occupation. This fact is so well known that I need say but a few words under this head. The report of deaths in this country for past years, speaks more plainly than any words of mine can do. Yet I will give what I think are a few of the reasons why this is so. One is, the farmer eats the fruit of his own hands; he knows that whatever food he produces is pure and unadulterated. The children of the farmer drink the pure milk from the farmer's cow. Another is, he follows in the fresh furrow of his plow. And how often do physicians prescribe for their patients this smell of the fresh earth. But the farmer's occupation supplies him with this. This, however, only applies to the male portion. Now I will prove that it is the most healthy for females. How often we find the daughters of professional men and mechanics, who would disdain to milk a cow, skim a pan of milk, or prepare a churning of butter for market, out of health, and on consulting a physician, are told that they must go on a journey to the springs, ride on horseback, or take other outdoor exercise; while the farmer's daughter, who cheerfully assists her mother in the kitchen, the dairy, and tending the poultry, never knows the need of such exercise.

Mr. President, allow me to relate an anecdote, which may be of service to some of the rising generation. It will show the young ladies how to reject one man and accept another. The heroine of this anecdote was a respectable farmer's daughter. A young man of her acquaintance called on her one evening, and made proposals of marriage. She told him that she wished until the next evening to decide. The following afternoon she told her father that she wanted the horse to go about two miles. At the appointed time the horse was saddled, and she mounted and rode off. On arriving at the place where she intended to stop, she saw that the great barn doors were open, and the old gentleman was pitching off a load of hay which stood on the barn floor. She rode up and inquired of him, "Where is your son Samuel?" "He is up on the mow, taking away the hay," was his answer. "I want to speak with him," said she. Sam then jumped from the mow on to the load of hay, by the side of his father. "You need not come any further," said she, "I can

say what I wish here; I have nothing private." She then told
him that she had received proposals of marriage from a
certain young man. "But," she said, "I have never seen any
one I love as I do you, and the last time we stood side by
side and read in the old schoolhouse, I made up my mind
that I never would give my heart and hand to any one until
I knew *you* would not accept them. Now," said she, "I want
to know whether you will marry me or not." The old
gentleman, unable to keep silent any longer, called out,
"take her Sam, take her, she'll make you a good one." The
young people exchanged a few words, when the old farmer,
in joy cried out, "it's a bargain, and I'm a happy witness.
God bless you, my children." The next evening, when the
young man came for his answer, she told him his offer was
an honorable one, and she thanked him for it; that she
should always respect him, and speak well of him to her
female acquaintances; but duty required her to give a negative answer. Now, this was a real farmers' courtship, and if
there were more like it, there would be fewer unhappy
marriages.

Since railroads have become so common and convenient,
I have noticed that some young ladies spend a great deal of
their time riding in the cars. Now, I know not what their
business is, neither do I expect to; but one thing I am quite
sure of, they are not like this young woman, in pursuit of a
farmer's son for a husband, and I have come to this conclusion, that if they would spend less of their time in this way,
and more of it in assisting their mothers in that portion of
farm work belonging to the female sex, they would be
healthier, happier, and in the married life more contented
with their husbands.

But the last and most important reason why farming is
healthy, perhaps, is his spending so great a proportion of
his time at work in the open air, which gives him a good
relish for his food, and strengthens his whole body.

Fourth. Farming is the most honorable occupation. God

himself is the author of it. We read in the Holy Scriptures, that "the Lord God planted a garden eastward in Eden," and "the Lord God took the man and put him into the garden to dress it and to keep it." Now, will any one be so impious as to say that an occupation is disrespectful that God himself is the author of? Will any mother teach her children that the first duty that God ever pointed out for man to perform was not honorable? Shall an occupation which feeds the whole world, and has, from the foundation of the world up to the present time, fed all the human race — shall such an occupation be called disrespectful? Not even the gospel of Jesus Christ could be preached among us without it. Is there any father, mother, son, or daughter, who would dare to stand up in this assembly and say that farming is dishonorable?

Friends, let us for a moment compare the employment of the farmer with that of the broker, who shaves notes in State street. We well know that a year or more past has been a busy time for this class of men. Suppose a broker executes his cunning faculties to their utmost ability, and shaves notes at an enormous interest. He feels that he has added greatly to his fortune; but when night comes, as he lays his head on his pillow, conscience asks him, What have you done today for the benefit of the human race? He is troubled for an answer, and turns over. But conscience again interrogates him — Have you done anything to relieve the wants of the suffering? Have you done anything toward feeding the fowls of the air, or the beasts of the fields? Have you done anything productive of man's happiness? Have you done anything for which the rising generation will rise up and call you blessed?

In answer to all these inquiries, conscience compels him to answer, "No," and he turns himself in bed, in hopes of going to sleep, but his dreams are troublesome.

Mr. President, we here see that for all this man's great day's work, the world is not one cent better off.

Let us now turn our attention to the farmer for a moment. Suppose he applies his wisdom, skill and strength to carry on his occupation. Where the brush was growing, the last time we saw the spot, today we see beautiful fields of grass and grain, growing for man and beast — all for the benefit of the whole human family. The farmer, also lays his head on the pillow at night, and in his mind reviews the labors of the day. His conscience approves every act, and says to him, "The earth rejoices in being able to produce food for man, where nothing but briars grew before." Nature smiles and man is blessed with the harvest; God is glorified in seeing man perform the first duty he assigned him, and by his blessing sanctions the declaration, that God, Nature and Man are co-workers in producing food and happiness for the whole family of man.

Mr. President, in conclusion, I would say, that at the beginning of farming God would not have planted a garden in Eden and put man in it, to dress and keep it, if He, in His infinite wisdom, had not foreseen that it would be a profitable, independent, healthy, honorable and happy employment for the human race.

If my hearers are not already tired, I would like to close with the following sentiment:

WOMAN — We honor her, because she is a free gift from God to man; we love her, because God, in all His work of creation, never has created a being more worthy of man's love.